ALGORITHM DIARIES

LIGHTHEARTED TAKE ON UNDERSTANDING DATA SCIENCE ALGORITHMS

KALICHARAN
MAHASIVABHATTU

To my loving children, Agastya and Nithya, who have been a constant source of inspiration and joy. Agastya, my 13-year-old son, whose own published work sparked my journey into writing, and Nithya, my precious daughter, whose love and affection know no bounds. This book is dedicated to you both, with endless gratitude and love

Contents

Preface   *vii*

Acknowledgements   *ix*

Prologue   *xi*

1. A Hilarious Guide To Data Science Jargon Jungle   1

2. Making Beach Decisions With Decision Trees   9

3. Traffic Jams And Honking K-nearest Neighbors   16

4. Award For Best Supporting Vector Goes To..   21

5. Cooking With The Naive Bayes Knowledge   26

6. Cricket Conversations: Exploring Linear And Polynomial Regressions   31

7. Party Probabilities: Unraveling The Sigmoid Function   38

8. Cluster Capers: Exploring K-means   43

9. Algorithm Avengers: Unleashing The Random Forests   49

10. Artful Dimensionality: Unraveling Pca   53

11. Branching Out With Hierarchical Clustering   59

12. Boosting Algorithms: The Flavors Of Teamwork   65

13. From Machine Learning To Deep Learning: A Futuristic Leap   70

14. Between Neurons And Networks   75

15. Picture Perfect: Demystifying Cnn's   80

16. Unlocking Memory's Mysteries: Dive Into Lstms   86

17. Generating Unseen Realities: The Power Of Gans   91

18. Reinforcement Love Through Trial, Error, And   97

Contents

Rewards

19. United By Data Science: A Promising Future   104
   Together

Thankyou   113

Preface

The genesis of "Algorithm Diaries" came to me as I observed the struggle many face in comprehending the increasingly complex world of machine learning and data science. For those without a strong technical background, the subject matter can seem overwhelming and, at times, even unapproachable. My goal in writing this book is to break down these barriers and provide a unique, accessible, and engaging exploration of the subject, free from the intimidating language that often accompanies technical texts.

In "Algorithm Diaries," readers are invited to join Prakash and Swetha, an endearing couple who share a passion for learning and a flair for humor. By employing a lighthearted and relatable narrative, I aimed to present each machine learning algorithm in a way that piques curiosity and inspires understanding. Using familiar, everyday situations as the backdrop for each chapter, the book demonstrates that even the most advanced concepts can be distilled into engaging, digestible pieces.

Although it may seem unconventional, I believe that the fusion of romance, humor, and education in this book serves as a potent reminder that learning can and should be enjoyable. Furthermore, it is my hope that readers will not only grasp the underlying principles of machine learning but also appreciate the value of humor and connection in the learning process.

Whether you are a novice eager to explore the world of data science or an experienced professional looking for a fresh take on the subject, "Algorithm Diaries" is designed to entertain, inform, and inspire. As you immerse yourself in the journey of Prakash and Swetha, may you find laughter, wisdom, and a newfound appreciation for the beauty and intricacy of machine learning algorithms.

Welcome to the captivating world of "Algorithm Diaries." Let the adventure begin.

Acknowledgements

Writing "Algorithm Diaries" has been an incredible journey, and there are many individuals whose support, encouragement, and insights have contributed significantly to its completion. I would like to express my deepest gratitude to all those who have been a part of this experience.

To my dear friends and colleagues, who have always believed in my abilities and pushed me to explore new avenues, I am truly grateful for your camaraderie and guidance. Your feedback and constructive criticism have been invaluable in shaping the final manuscript.

I would also like to extend my gratitude to the countless authors, researchers, and pioneers in the field of machine learning and data science. Your groundbreaking work and dedication to advancing our collective understanding have laid the foundation for this book.

To my editor and the entire publishing team, your diligence, professionalism, and expertise have transformed my manuscript into a polished and engaging final product. Your enthusiasm for the project and attention to detail have been truly exceptional.

Finally, I want to express my heartfelt appreciation to you, the reader, for embarking on this journey with me. It is my sincerest hope that "Algorithm Diaries" brings you as much joy and enlightenment as it has brought me in writing it. Here's to discovering the magic of machine learning, one feel-good algorithm at a time.

Prakash and Swetha, two young professionals in the bustling IT hub of Bangalore, were always eager to stay ahead in their fast-paced industry. Prakash, a seasoned web developer with a strong foundation in Java, had a keen eye for detail and a passion for innovation. Swetha, on the other hand, was a talented business analyst with a knack for identifying opportunities and driving strategic decisions. Though they worked in the same company and were dating each other, their individual skill sets seemed to set them on distinct paths. However, as the world of technology evolved and the buzz around AI grew louder, Prakash and Swetha began to consider the potential of data science in their respective careers. Fueled by curiosity and a shared determination to learn, they embarked on a journey that would not only strengthen their bond but also reshape their professional futures in ways they could never have imagined.

On a Monday morning, Prakash and Swetha were enjoying a cup of coffee in the office cafeteria, taking a break from their hectic work routine. They had been dating for a while, and their shared passion for the IT industry had brought them closer.

Prakash sighed, "You know, Swetha, I've been thinking about making a move to a new company. I feel like my skills are becoming outdated. There's so much buzz about AI and data science, and I'm not sure how much longer my web development experience will be relevant."

Swetha nodded sympathetically. "I understand where you're coming from. I've also been considering a change. My boss is so micromanaging, and it's driving me crazy.

But I'm not sure if data science is for me, you know? I'm a business analyst, not a programmer."

Prakash nodded and reassured Swetha, saying, "I see what you mean, but don't worry! A career in AI can be a great fit for a business analyst too. In fact, your background in understanding business processes and requirements can be a valuable asset in the AI field."

He continued, "Data science and AI are all about solving problems and making data-driven decisions. As a business analyst, you already have experience in identifying issues, analyzing data, and providing recommendations. With some additional training in AI and data science techniques, you can apply those skills to even more complex problems and add value to your team."

Swetha added, "I've glanced at some of the courses, and they seemed to be so extensive. I'm not sure if I have the technical mindset to grasp all that material."

Prakash took a sip of his coffee, then a thought struck him. "Hey, what if we both try learning data science together? We could make it fun and engaging by learning the algorithms and explaining them to each other using real-life examples."

Swetha raised her eyebrows, intrigued by the proposal. "That actually sounds interesting. It would be a great way to learn, laugh, and spend time together. I'm in!"

Prakash smiled, and they clinked their coffee mugs together in agreement. Thus began their exciting journey into the world of data science, as a team.

1

A Hilarious Guide to Data Science Jargon Jungle

Prakash and Swetha were excited to start their journey into machine learning. They had ordered books on the subject from Amazon and spent two weeks individually learning the basics. Now, they were eager to share their newfound knowledge with each other in a simplified manner, using everyday objects as examples.

They met up at a cozy coffee shop and eagerly pulled out their notebooks to discuss their progress.

"So, Swetha," Prakash began, "how would you explain machine learning using everyday objects?"

Swetha thought for a moment and then said, "Imagine our coffee maker at home. It's a simple machine that makes coffee, right? Now, think of machine learning as a smart coffee maker. Instead of just brewing coffee, it can learn from our preferences, like how strong we want our coffee or what time we usually have it. Over time, it adapts and

"

makes the perfect cup of coffee for us, without us having to tell it every single detail."

Prakash nodded in agreement. "That's a great example. Here's another one. You know how our smartphones have predictive text features? That's an application of machine learning. Our phones learn from our texting patterns and suggest words based on what we're most likely to type next."

Swetha smiled. "Exactly! And the more we use it, the better it gets at predicting what we want to say."

Prakash flipped through the pages of his machine learning book, eager to share some important terms with Swetha. He began reading out some key concepts and their definitions, ensuring that they both had a solid understanding of the terminology before diving into specific algorithms.

Prakash, with a serious look on his face " So are you sure you figured the terms such as Dataset, Model, Overfitting, Gradient descent, Hyperparameters..."

Swetha suddenly interrupted Prakash's recitation of machine learning terms with a playful grin. "Hold on, Prakash! This isn't the fun learning experience we wanted. Let's make it more interesting," she suggested.

Prakash raised his eyebrows curiously, wondering what Swetha had in mind.

"How about this," Swetha continued, "I'll skim through the book, pick a term, and then you have to come up with a hilarious way to explain it. After that, you do the same for me. Let's make learning these terms a real laugh!"

Prakash chuckled and agreed. "That sounds like a brilliant idea, Swetha. Let's give it a shot!"

Swetha flipped through her book, found a term, and said, "Alright, here's your first challenge: **Dataset.**'"

Prakash thought for a moment before coming up with a humorous way to explain 'dataset.' He grinned and said, "Alright, imagine a dataset as a party. You've got all kinds of guests mingling, from the tall ones to the short ones, the loud talkers to the shy ones, and everything in between. Now, each guest represents a data point, and their unique attributes are the features. The more diverse the party guests, the more interesting the party, just like a rich dataset makes for better machine learning!"

Swetha couldn't help but laugh at Prakash's amusing analogy. Her eyes sparkled with amusement as she said, "Oh, that's a brilliant way to put it, Prakash! It makes datasets sound like so much fun, and I can clearly visualize all those quirky party guests."

Swetha asked Prakash, "Let's see if can you explain the difference between **classification** and **regression** in a similar way!"

"Alright, let me give it a shot! Imagine you're at a magical fruit market, and you have two tasks. In the first task, which is like classification, you have to sort all the fruits into different baskets based on their type – apples, oranges, bananas, and so on. It's all about putting them into the right categories."

He continued, "Now, for the second task, which is like regression, things get a bit more... magical. Instead of sorting the fruits, you have to predict the exact weight of each fruit just by looking at it! It's not about categories anymore; it's about finding a precise value for each individual fruit."

Prakash flipped through his book, eager to challenge Swetha. "Alright, Swetha, your turn. Let's see if you can explain **'training set'** and **'testing set'**"

Swetha thought for a moment, then her face lit up with an idea. "Okay, let's think of machine learning as a baking competition. The 'training set' is like the practice sessions where the contestants experiment with different recipes and techniques. They learn from their mistakes, and eventually, they come up with the perfect cake."

She continued, "Now, the 'testing set' is like the actual competition day. The contestants have to bake their best cake using the skills they acquired during their practice sessions. The judges evaluate their performance and declare the winner. In the same way, a machine learning model uses the testing set to prove how well it learned from the training set and how accurate its predictions are!"

Prakash listened attentively, and as Swetha finished her explanation, he broke into a wide grin. "Swetha, that's a fantastic analogy! You've managed to convey the essence of training and testing sets in such an entertaining and easily digestible way. I must admit, you're not bad at this either!"

Swetha glanced at her book, searching for another term to challenge Prakash. "Your next term is **'Loss Function.'** Give me a fun explanation, Prakash!"

Prakash pondered for a moment before his eyes sparkled. "Alright, imagine you're playing darts at a pub. The goal is to hit the bullseye, but let's face it, not all of us are expert dart players. So, the 'Loss Function' is like the distance between where your dart lands and the bullseye. Your aim is to minimize that distance to become a better player, just like a machine learning model aims to minimize the loss function to make better predictions!"

Prakash flipped through his book , ready to challenge Swetha again. "I've got two terms for you: **'Model'** and **'Target Variable.'** Give me your funniest explanation!"

Swetha thought for a moment and then smiled as she came up with a creative thought. "Okay, think of the 'Model' as a fortune-teller and the 'Target Variable' as the prediction they're trying to make. The fortune-teller takes all the information available, like the client's birthdate, star sign, and favorite color, to predict their future. In machine learning, the model does the same thing! It takes all the input features and uses them to predict the target variable, whether it's the price of a house, the winner of a sports match, or the best restaurant to go to on a Friday night!"

Swetha smirked as she scanned her book . "Okay, Prakash, let's see if you can come up with an explanation for **'Supervised and Unsupervised Learning'**"

Prakash devised a creative analogy. "Well, Supervised learning is like having a strict teacher who guides you every step of the way. They tell you what to do, how to do it, and correct your mistakes along the way. It's like having a GPS navigator that constantly tells you where to go and when to turn. You might feel a little suffocated, but hey, at least you won't get lost!

On the other hand, Unsupervised learning is like wandering around in a new city without a map or a guide. You have no idea where you're going or what you're doing, but you're free to explore and make your own discoveries. It's like being a toddler who's just learning to walk - you'll stumble and fall a few times, but eventually, you'll figure things out on your own."

Prakash continued "Alright, Swetha, let's see how you can explain **'Epoch'** and **'Batch'** in a fun way!"

Swetha thought for a moment, then smiled as she came up with an engaging analogy. "Okay, let's imagine machine learning as a fitness boot camp. Each 'Epoch' is like a full workout session where every participant goes through all the exercises at least once. They learn from their mistakes and improve their technique during each session."

She continued, "Now, 'Batch' is like dividing the participants into smaller groups. Instead of the trainer focusing on everyone at once, they can give more attention to each group, making the training more efficient. In machine learning, we divide the training data into smaller batches and update the model incrementally, speeding up the learning process and making it more manageable."

Swetha looked at her book with a mischievous smile, "Alright, Prakash, I've got a term for you: '**Overfitting**.' Let's hear your explanation!"

Prakash thought for a moment, "Okay, let's say you're trying to impress someone with your dance moves. You practice a lot, and you get really good at dancing... in your bedroom. You're able to match every little bump and groove in the floor. But when you finally take your dance moves to a party, you realize they don't work as well on a different floor with different imperfections."

He continued, "That's what 'Overfitting' is like in machine learning. The model gets so good at fitting the training data that it captures all its noise and irregularities, but when it's time to make predictions on new, unseen data, it performs poorly because it's too focused on the specific quirks of the training data."

Prakash"Alright, Swetha, '**Regularization**' "

Swetha pondered for a moment "Okay, think of a machine learning model as a person who's trying to lose weight. They have a workout routine, but they tend to overdo it and get injured, or they're too focused on just one exercise, neglecting other important muscle groups."

She continued, "Now, 'Regularization' is like adding a personal trainer to the mix. The trainer helps the person find balance in their workout, ensuring they don't overdo it in any one area and maintaining a well-rounded fitness routine. In machine learning, regularization is a technique that adds a penalty term to the loss function, preventing the model from focusing too much on specific features or fitting the training data too closely, which helps avoid overfitting."

"Okay, Prakash, your next term is '**Noise in Data**.' Give me your weird explanation!"

Prakash came up with a one more. "Alright, imagine you're at a party, and the music is pumping. Everyone's having a great time, dancing and chatting, but you're trying to have a conversation with someone. The loud music, laughter, and chatter from the other guests make it hard to hear what the person is saying. That's what 'Noise in Data' is like!"

He continued, "In a dataset, noise refers to the random, irrelevant, or inconsistent information that makes it difficult for a machine learning model to understand the true patterns and relationships between variables. Just like at the party, the noise in the data can drown out the important information we're trying to uncover."

Prakash and Swetha looked at each other, feeling satisfied with their progress. They had covered a lot of machine learning terminology in a fun and engaging manner.

Prakash stretched and said, "I think we've covered a lot today, and we've had a great time doing it! What do you say? We take a break now and start discussing the algorithms next week?"

Swetha nodded, smiling. "I agree, we've made great progress, and it's been so much fun! Let's take a break and come back refreshed next week, ready to dive into the algorithms."

Both of them felt a sense of accomplishment and excitement about their unique approach to learning machine learning concepts. They knew they had set a strong foundation for their learning journey, and they eagerly looked forward to discovering and discussing the algorithms in the coming weeks.

2

Making Beach Decisions with Decision Trees

On a balmy Saturday evening, Swetha and Prakash sat on the beach, their eyes fixed on the endless waves. The beach was alive with people, as hawkers weaved their way through the crowds, selling all manner of wares. Despite the hustle and bustle, a sense of serenity prevailed, casting a peaceful spell over the scene.

Prakash: "Hey Swetha, do you know what decision trees are in the world of data science?"

Swetha: "No, not really. I haven't read that one yet. What's that?"

Prakash: "Well, decision trees are actually not that complicated. Think of them as a series of yes or no questions that help you make a decision. In data science, they're used for classification and regression tasks. Let's take an example here at the beach."

Swetha: "Okay, I'm listening."

Prakash: "Imagine you want to predict whether someone will buy a coconut from a hawker or not. A decision tree could help with that. You start at the top with a simple question like, 'Is the person thirsty?' If yes, you move to the next question, 'Do they have cash?' If yes again, you might predict they'll buy a coconut. If not at any point, they probably won't."

Swetha: "Hmm, interesting. But how does the tree know which questions to ask?"

Prakash: "Alright, let me explain using an example dataset. Let's say we have data on 100 people at the beach and whether they bought coconuts or not. We also have information about each person's thirstiness, cash availability, and whether they like coconuts. The data might look something like this:

Person 1: Thirsty, Has Cash, Likes Coconuts, Bought Coconut

Person 2: Not Thirsty, No Cash, Likes Coconuts, Didn't Buy Coconut

Person 3: Thirsty, Has Cash, Doesn't Like Coconuts, Didn't Buy Coconut

...

Person 100: Thirsty, No Cash, Likes Coconuts, Didn't Buy Coconut

When constructing the decision tree, we want to find the factors that best split the data into groups with similar outcomes (i.e., bought or didn't buy a coconut). We can calculate a metric called 'information gain' for each factor, which tells us how well it splits the data.

Swetha, feeling a bit overwhelmed, asked, "This is confusing. Can you explain information gain in a more simple language and maybe use the same example?"

Prakash: "Of course, let me break it down for you. Information gain is essentially about finding the feature that creates the most 'order' or 'purity' in our dataset when splitting it. It helps us understand which feature is the best at separating the groups based on the target variable. In our beach example, we want to know which factor – thirstiness, cash availability, or liking coconuts – is the most helpful in determining whether someone buys a coconut or not."

He continued, "Imagine we first split the data based on thirstiness. We might find that, among the thirsty people, 80% bought coconuts, while among the not-thirsty people, only 20% bought coconuts. This split provides some useful information, but let's try splitting based on cash availability."

Prakash went on, "When we split the data based on cash availability, we find that 90% of people with cash bought coconuts, while only 10% without cash did. This split appears to be more informative than the one based on thirstiness. So, the information gain for cash availability would be higher than for thirstiness."

Swetha nodded, starting to understand the concept more clearly. "Ah, I see. So, information gain helps us find the most useful feature to split the data on for our decision tree, right?"

Prakash smiled, "Exactly! You got it. It helps us identify the best feature to separate the groups in our dataset, making the decision tree more effective at predicting outcomes."

In our example, let's say we find the following information gains:

Thirstiness: 0.4

Cash Availability: 0.6

Liking Coconuts: 0.3

Since 'cash availability' has the highest information gain, we'll use that as the first question in our decision tree. So, the tree would start with 'Does the person have cash?'

Next, we'd look at the remaining factors for each group (cash and no cash). In the 'cash' group, we might find that 'thirsty' has the highest information gain, so we'd ask 'Are they thirsty?' as the next question in that branch. Similarly, we'd choose the best factor for the 'no cash' group and continue building the tree this way.

The tree stops growing when it reaches a certain depth or when the information gain for further splits is too small. This helps prevent overfitting, which means making the model too complex and sensitive to noise in the data."

Swetha: "Wow, that makes a lot of sense! So the decision tree is all about finding the factors that best separate the data based on the outcome. I think I'm getting the hang of this!"

As they continued their conversation, a hawker approached them, selling sunglasses.

Hawker: "Hey there! Would you like to buy some sunglasses? They're perfect for this sunny day!"

Swetha: (smirking) "Perfect timing! Let's test the decision tree concept. Prakash, should I buy these sunglasses?"

Prakash: (laughing) "Alright, let's give it a try. First question: 'Is it sunny?'"

Swetha: "Well, it's a bit cloudy, so I'll say no."

Prakash: "Okay, let's move to the next question: 'Do you like the design of the sunglasses?'"

Swetha: "Hmm, they're not bad, so I'll say yes."

Prakash: "Great! Next question: 'Are they within your budget?'"

Swetha: "Yes, they are affordable."

Prakash: "Alright, let's consider another factor: 'Do you already own a pair of sunglasses?'"

Swetha: "Yes, I do."

Prakash: "And the final question: 'Are your current sunglasses damaged or in need of replacement?'"

Swetha: "No, they're still in good condition."

Prakash: "Based on your answers, I'd predict that you probably won't buy these sunglasses, since it's not sunny and you already have a good pair."

Swetha: "You're right! Sorry, Mr. Hawker, not today."

Hawker: (grinning) "No worries, have a great day!"

As the hawker moved on, Swetha turned to Prakash, impressed by the decision tree analysis.

Swetha: "This is fascinating, Prakash! But I'm curious, are there any cases where decision trees might not be the best choice?"

Prakash: "Great question, Swetha! Decision trees do have some limitations. Here are a few situations where they might not be the best choice:

Noisy data: Decision trees can be sensitive to small fluctuations or noise in the data. They might create complex trees that fit the noise instead of the underlying trend, which is called overfitting. In such cases, more robust models, like ensemble methods or neural networks, could be better options.

Continuous variables: While decision trees can handle continuous variables, they're not as efficient as some other algorithms like linear regression or support vector machines. Decision trees will split continuous variables into discrete categories, which can lead to a loss of information.

High-dimensional data: If you have a large number of input features, decision trees can become very deep and complex, making them harder to interpret and more prone to overfitting. In these situations, dimensionality reduction techniques or other algorithms like support vector machines or deep learning might be more suitable.

Complex relationships: Decision trees work best when the relationship between input features and the output is relatively simple. If there are complex, non-linear relationships, or if the interactions between features are important, other algorithms like neural networks or kernel-based methods might be more effective.

Inherent imbalance: In cases where there's a significant imbalance in the outcome classes, decision trees can struggle to make accurate predictions. Techniques like oversampling, undersampling, or using different algorithms like random forests, which are more robust to class imbalance, might be preferable."

Swetha: "I see, so decision trees have their limitations, and we should choose our algorithm based on the specific problem and dataset we're working with. Thanks for the insights, Prakash!"

Prakash: "Exactly, Swetha! There's no one-size-fits-all solution in data science. It's all about understanding the problem, the data, and the trade-offs between different algorithms to make the best choice for your specific situation."

Swetha: "I see. Thanks for explaining, Prakash. It's not as complicated as I thought! Can you give some real-world examples too?"

Prakash: "Certainly, Swetha! One real-world example where decision trees have been successfully used is in credit risk assessment by financial institutions. Banks and other lenders use decision trees to evaluate the creditworthiness of loan applicants.

In this case, the decision tree model is trained on historical data of borrowers, including information like their credit score, employment status, income level, outstanding debts, and loan repayment history. The output variable is whether the borrower defaulted on the loan or not.

By constructing a decision tree based on these features, the bank can predict the likelihood of a new applicant defaulting on a loan. This helps them make informed decisions on whether to approve or reject loan applications, as well as determine appropriate interest rates and loan terms.

The use of decision trees in credit risk assessment has been quite popular due to their simplicity, interpretability, and ease of implementation. The model can be easily explained to regulators and stakeholders, and it can be quickly updated with new data to ensure its accuracy over time."

Swetha: "That's a great example, Prakash! It really helps me see how decision trees can be applied in real-world situations. Thanks for sharing!"

Prakash: "You're welcome, Swetha! Remember, even the most complex concepts can be understood with the right examples and a dash of humor."

3

Traffic Jams and honking K-Nearest Neighbors

It was another dreary Monday morning in Bangalore, India, and Prakash and Swetha were on their way to work in Swetha's car. The roads were choked with traffic, as usual, and the cacophony of horns blaring and engines revving filled the air.

As they were waiting at the red-light signal, Swetha turned towards Prakash and said, "You know, I've been reading up on machine learning algorithms too."

Prakash was surprised and delighted. "That's great! Which algorithm have you been exploring?

"I've been reading about the k-nearest neighbors algorithm," Swetha replied. "It's fascinating how it can be used for both classification and regression problems."

Swetha grinned as a sudden honk from a nearby vehicle interrupted her thoughts. "Speaking of k-nearest neighbors, I feel like this traffic is an interesting example," she said.

Prakash raised his eyebrows, intrigued. "Oh? How so?"

"Well, think about it," Swetha explained, gesturing at the cars around them. "Imagine each car as a data point in a multi-dimensional space. The features could be things like size, speed, or even driver temperament."

As if on cue, a loud honk echoed from behind them, causing both of them to jump. Prakash chuckled, "Driver temperament definitely seems important."

Swetha laughed, "Absolutely! So, using the k-nearest neighbors algorithm, we could predict something like the likelihood of a car honking, based on the characteristics of its k-nearest neighbors. In other words, if the cars with similar features around you are honking, it's more likely you'll honk too."

Prakash was surprised and asked. "No way, why would I honk? I don't think I am their neighbor. Maybe on a location basis I am closer to them but not when you consider other dimensions."

Swetha nodded in agreement. "You're right, Prakash. Just being in the vicinity of honking cars doesn't necessarily mean that you'll honk too. That's where the distance metric comes into play. In k-nearest neighbors, the algorithm calculates the distance between each feature like the size, speed and driver temperament to determine which points are actually neighbors."

Prakash looked thoughtful. "So, how does the algorithm measure the distance between these multi-dimensional data points?"

Swetha smiled, excited to explain further. "There are several ways to measure distance, but one of the most common methods is the Euclidean distance. It's basically the straight-line distance between two points in a multi-dimensional space. The formula for Euclidean distance is the square root of the sum of the squared differences between corresponding coordinates of the two points."

Prakash furrowed his brow. "Okay, I think I get it. So, in our traffic example, the algorithm would calculate the Euclidean distance between each car based on their features like size, speed, and driver temperament, right?"

"Exactly," Swetha confirmed. "And by considering these features, we can find the cars that are not just spatially close, but also similar in other aspects. This makes the prediction more meaningful and accurate. Of course, there are other distance metrics as well, like Manhattan distance or Minkowski distance, which could be used depending on the problem you're trying to solve."

Prakash nodded, understanding the concept better. "So, by measuring the distance between data points in multiple dimensions, we can find neighbors that are more likely to share similar characteristics, and not just based on their location. That's fascinating!"

Prakash thought for a moment and asked, "But how do you choose the value of k? Is there a rule of thumb?"

Swetha nodded. "There isn't a one-size-fits-all answer, but a common approach is to use cross-validation. You test the algorithm with different values of k and choose the one that gives you the best results. Sometimes, using odd values for k is preferred to avoid ties."

Prakash asked, "Swetha, I've heard that KNN doesn't really 'learn' anything as a model and just tries to run predictions each time. In what aspects is this algorithm different from others?"

Swetha nodded, acknowledging the question. "That's a great observation, Prakash. The k-nearest neighbors algorithm is an instance-based or lazy learning algorithm. Unlike other algorithms that build a model during the training phase, KNN doesn't have an explicit training step. Instead, it stores the entire training dataset in memory, and during the prediction phase, it calculates the distance between the new data point and all stored data points to find the k-nearest neighbors."

Prakash looked curious. "So, does that mean it's less efficient compared to other algorithms?"

Swetha considered the question for a moment. "In a way, yes. KNN can be computationally expensive, particularly when dealing with large datasets, since it calculates distances on the fly during the prediction phase. This can slow down the process, making it less suitable for some real-time applications. However, one advantage of KNN is that it's more adaptable to changes in the data. Since it doesn't build a model during training, it can incorporate new data points easily."

Prakash nodded thoughtfully. "I see. So, while it might not be the best choice for all situations, it could still be useful for specific problems or when dealing with dynamic datasets."

Prakash, now intrigued by the k-nearest neighbors algorithm, asked, "Swetha, can you give some real-world examples where KNN is a great choice?"

Swetha thought for a moment before responding, "Sure, Prakash! KNN can be particularly useful in a variety of situations. Let me give you a few examples."

She continued, "One area where KNN is commonly used is in recommendation systems. For instance, say you have a movie streaming platform. You can use KNN to find users with similar tastes based on their movie ratings, and then recommend movies that these similar users have enjoyed. This is known as collaborative filtering."

Prakash nodded, finding the example relatable. "Ah, that makes sense. It's like having a group of friends who recommend movies based on your shared interests."

"Exactly," Swetha agreed. "Another example is in healthcare, where KNN can be used to predict the diagnosis of a patient based on their medical data. By finding patients with similar symptoms and medical histories, KNN can help identify trends and suggest possible diagnoses."

Prakash looked impressed. "Wow, I didn't realize KNN could be so versatile."

Swetha smiled, glad to see Prakash's enthusiasm. "Definitely! And one more example is in the field of pattern recognition. KNN can be used for tasks like handwriting recognition or even image classification. By comparing a new image to a database of labeled images, KNN can predict the most likely class for the new image based on its k-nearest neighbors."

As they slowly inched forward in the traffic, another honk rang out, prompting Prakash to joke, "Maybe we should build a k-nearest neighbors model to predict which driver will honk next."

Swetha chuckled, "That could be our next startup idea – HonkPredict! We'll revolutionize driving in India."

They shared a laugh as the light turned green, and the cacophony of horns resumed. Though the traffic remained chaotic, the conversation about machine learning made their Monday morning commute just a bit more bearable.

4

Award for Best Supporting Vector goes to..

As Prakash and Swetha settled into their seats in the movie theatre, they eagerly awaited the start of the film. However, to their disappointment, the screen was filled with a series of advertisements that seemed to go on and on. Frustrated with the delay, they began discussing machine learning algorithms and their potential applications in the movie industry to pass the time. As another ad played out on the screen, they began to delve into a conversation about the potential applications of machine learning in the movie industry.

Prakash: (whispers) Hey Swetha, have you ever thought about how SVM can be applied in the movie industry?

Swetha: (whispers back, surprised) What? Why are you talking about this in a movie theatre? Shouldn't we be enjoying the movie?

Prakash: (whispers) I know, I know, but hear me out. Support Vector Machines can actually be used in the movie industry to predict box office success based on various factors like the genre, the cast, the budget, and so on.

Swetha: (whispers back, still hesitant) I don't know if I really want to talk about work stuff right now, especially here, now.

Prakash: (whispers) I understand, but this is really interesting! I promise it won't take long. We can continue talking about it after the movie if you want.

Swetha: (whispers back, finally convinced) Okay, fine. Looks like I don't have an option either.

Prakash: (whispers) Sure. So, imagine a scenario where a production house wants to predict the success of a movie before releasing it. They can use SVM to analyze the past box office data and predict the likelihood of success for a new movie.

Swetha finally realizes that they are both whispering for no reason as the audience is all talking anyways.

Swetha: Ah, I see. But how would they decide on the features to be used in the analysis?

Prakash: Good question. They can consider various factors such as the genre of the movie, the lead actors, the director, the budget, the release date, and so on. By analysing these features, they can predict the success rate of the movie.

Swetha: That's really interesting. SVM can be really useful in predicting the box office performance of movies.

Prakash continues, "Alright, so SVM, or Support Vector Machine, is a way to classify data by finding the best possible line or boundary to separate different classes."

Swetha interrupts, "Can you explain what you mean by a boundary line?"

Prakash replies, "Certainly! A boundary line is a line or surface that acts as a separator between different classes of data points. In our movie example, imagine plotting all the movies on a graph with their characteristics. The boundary line is the best possible line we can draw to separate hit movies from flops, so that most of the hits are on one side and most of the flops are on the other. This line helps the SVM model make accurate predictions about whether a new movie will be a hit or a flop based on its characteristics."

Swetha nods her head, "Okay, that makes sense. So SVM can divide the movie dataset into two groups."

Prakash adds, "Exactly! And the best part is that it can also help in optimizing the marketing and advertising strategies for the movie, based on its predicted success rate. This way, the producers can make informed decisions about how much money they should spend on promotions and where to target their ads."

Swetha chimes in, "That's really interesting. But how does SVM actually determine the best boundary line?"

Prakash replies, "Well, SVM uses a mathematical approach to find the line that maximizes the distance between the different classes of data points. This line is called the 'margin', and the data points that are closest to this margin are called the 'support vectors'. By finding the best margin and support vectors, SVM can accurately classify new data points."

Swetha: Prakash, I understood how SVM works, but how is it different from other algorithms like KNN and Decision Trees?

Prakash: That's a good question, Swetha. One major difference between SVM and KNN is that SVM tries to find the best possible boundary that separates the two classes, whereas KNN simply classifies a new data point based on the majority of its k-nearest neighbours.

Swetha: Hmm, I see. And what about Decision Trees?

Prakash: Decision Trees create a tree-like model of decisions and their possible consequences. It tries to create the most optimal tree that splits the data based on the features that are most informative for classification. SVM, on the other hand, tries to find the most optimal hyperplane that separates the classes.

Swetha: Okay, I think I understand the differences now. But which algorithm is better?

Prakash: It really depends on the data and the problem we're trying to solve. In some cases, KNN may be better suited, while in others, SVM may outperform the rest. It's always important to try different algorithms and see which one performs the best on our specific dataset.

Swetha: Okay, I see. Can you give me an example of a scenario where SVM is a better choice compared to other algorithms?

Prakash: Sure, let's say we have a dataset that has a lot of features, and these features have a lot of noise. In this case, using other algorithms like logistic regression or decision trees might lead to overfitting or underfitting, as they try to fit the data to a specific model. However, SVM tries to find the best hyperplane that separates the data, which reduces the impact of noise and results in a better classification model.

Swetha: I see, so SVM is more robust in handling noisy data compared to other algorithms.

Prakash: Exactly, and not just that, SVM is also effective in handling non-linearly separable data. It uses a technique called kernel trick to transform the data to a higher-dimensional space where it becomes linearly separable.

Swetha: Yikes, that's too complex for me to understand. Can you please explain in simpler English please.

Prakash: Sure, let me explain in simpler terms. Imagine we have data that cannot be separated by a straight line in a two-dimensional space. SVM takes this data and transforms it into a higher-dimensional space where it becomes easier to separate. It's like moving the data to a different dimension where we can draw a straight line to separate it.

Swetha: Oh, I see. So it's like taking a problem that can't be solved and making it solvable by changing the perspective?

Prakash: Exactly! SVM uses the kernel trick to change the perspective and make the problem solvable.

Swetha: That's interesting. So, SVM is useful when we have a lot of noisy data or when the data is not linearly separable.

Prakash: Yes, and another advantage of SVM is that it has a regularization parameter which helps in preventing overfitting. This allows SVM to generalize well on new and unseen data.

Swetha: I see, so SVM has multiple advantages that make it a better choice for certain types of datasets.

Prakash: Yes, exactly. That's why it's important to understand the characteristics of the dataset and the strengths and weaknesses of different algorithms before choosing the best one for the task at hand.

Swetha smiles, "Wow, I'm really glad we had this conversation. I learned a lot about SVM today."

Prakash grins, "Me too! And who knows, maybe one day we'll be using SVM to predict the best supporting Vector, sorry actor for the Oscars."

They both chuckle as the movie begins.

5

Cooking with the Naive Bayes knowledge

Prakash and Swetha are in the kitchen, cooking up a storm for their weekend dinner. The aroma of spices and the sizzling sound of food in the pan fills the air. Prakash is elbow-deep in soapy water, scrubbing dishes as Swetha chops vegetables with the precision of a skilled chef.

Swetha: (grinning) "Hey Prakash, since we're already multitasking here, what do you think about discussing an ML algorithm to spice things up?"

Prakash: (laughs) "You know what? Why not! We're already making magic in the kitchen, so let's cook up some knowledge too. What's on the menu, Chef Swetha?"

Swetha: "Alright, Sous-chef Prakash, I present to you... the Naive Bayes Algorithm! It's a classic dish in the world of machine learning, known for its simplicity and deliciously good results."

Prakash: (playfully) "Oh, I'm intrigued! But can you explain it to me as if I were a potato peeler? You know, simple and to the point."

Swetha: (chuckles) "Okay, Mr. Potato Peeler. Naive Bayes is a classification algorithm based on Bayes' theorem, which helps us find the probability of an event given some conditions. It's called 'naive' because it assumes that all the features in a dataset are independent of each other, which, as you know, is rarely the case in the real world."

Prakash: (nodding) "Ah, I see. So we're dealing with a simple-minded yet effective algorithm, eh? But how does it work in practice? Can you give me an appetizing example?"

Swetha: "Sure thing! Let's say we're running a fancy restaurant and want to predict whether a customer will order dessert or not based on factors like their age, dietary preferences, and the day of the week. We can use the Naive Bayes Algorithm to make this prediction by calculating the probability of each factor contributing to the decision and then combining these probabilities to find the overall probability."

Prakash: (waving a soapy spoon) "Hold up, Swetha! I'm going to need a little more flavor on this one. Can you dish out some actual probability numbers to help me digest the concept better?"

Swetha: (chuckles) "Of course, Prakash! Imagine we have a dataset with 100 customers. Let's say 60 of them ordered dessert. Now, out of these 60 dessert-ordering customers, 40 are below the age of 30, 30 have a sweet tooth, and 20 visit on weekends. We want to find the probability of a customer below 30, with a sweet tooth, ordering dessert on a weekend."

Prakash: (nodding) "Alright, I'm following you so far. What's next?"

Swetha: "First, we'll calculate the probability of each factor, given that a customer orders dessert. So, we have $P(Age<30|Dessert) = 40/60$, $P(SweetTooth|Dessert) = 30/60$, and P(Weekend|Dessert) = 20/60. We also need the probability of a customer ordering dessert, which is P(Dessert) = 60/100."

Prakash: "Got it! So now we just mix those probabilities together, right?"

Swetha: (grinning) "Almost! We'll multiply the probabilities together, and then multiply by the probability of ordering dessert. So, it's P(Age<30|Dessert) * P(SweetTooth|Dessert) * P(Weekend|Dessert) * P(Dessert). This gives us the probability of a customer with these factors ordering dessert. Of course, we'd also have to calculate the probability of them not ordering dessert and compare the two to make a final prediction."

Prakash: (grinning) "I like it! So it's like creating the perfect dessert by combining the right ingredients. But I have to ask, what's the catch? There must be some limitations to our naive little friend."

Swetha: "Well, since it assumes that all the features are independent, it might not be the best choice for datasets where the features have strong relationships. In those cases, our naive friend might get a little confused and not deliver the best results."

Prakash: (scratching his head) "Hold on, Swetha. Can you help me understand this 'independent' concept a bit more? Maybe toss in an example to make it stick?"

Swetha: (smiling) "Imagine we have a dataset with features like 'umbrella usage' and 'rain occurrence.' In reality, these two features are closely related because people are more likely to use umbrellas when it's raining. However, the Naive Bayes Algorithm would treat them as completely independent, as if one has no influence over the other. This could lead to some wonky predictions in certain scenarios."

Prakash: (grinning) "Ah, I get it now! It's like assuming the saltiness of my fries has nothing to do with how much salt I sprinkle on them. Quite the oversight, but I can see how it keeps the algorithm simple."

Swetha: "The assumption of independence is a trade-off that makes the algorithm easier to understand and compute. But when you need something more sophisticated, you might want to consider other algorithms that can handle these relationships more effectively."

Prakash: (raising an eyebrow) "Interesting! So, can you give me some examples of scenarios where Naive Bayes outshines other algorithms? When should I set the table with Naive Bayes as the main course?"

Swetha: (grinning) "Absolutely! There are a few tasty scenarios where Naive Bayes can be your go-to algorithm:

Text classification: Naive Bayes is a popular choice for tasks like spam detection or sentiment analysis. It works well with high-dimensional datasets, like word counts, where the features are often independent.

Real-time predictions: Since Naive Bayes is computationally efficient, it's great for situations where you need fast predictions, like in real-time recommendation systems or detecting fraudulent transactions.

Small datasets: Naive Bayes can perform reasonably well even with a limited amount of data, making it a suitable option when you don't have a large dataset to train on.

Multi-class problems: When you have multiple classes to predict, Naive Bayes can be a solid choice, as it can easily handle such scenarios without breaking a sweat."

Prakash: (nodding) "I see! So, it's like Naive Bayes is that versatile ingredient you can always rely on to add flavor to your machine learning recipes."

Swetha: "That's right, Prakash! While it might not always be the star of the show, Naive Bayes is a handy tool to have in your machine learning kitchen. Sometimes, simplicity and efficiency are just what you need to cook up the perfect solution."

Prakash: "True that, Swetha! Thanks for serving up this tasty morsel of knowledge. Now let's get back to our dinner and make sure it doesn't turn into a burnt offering!"

As they continue cooking, Prakash and Swetha share a hearty laugh, their newfound knowledge of the Naive Bayes Algorithm adding a delightful flavor to their culinary adventure.

6

Cricket Conversations: Exploring Linear and Polynomial regressions

Prakash and Swetha were sitting in a packed cricket stadium, surrounded by excited fans cheering for their local team. The match had been thrilling so far, but as the pace slowed down, the atmosphere became a bit dull. To bring some excitement back into their conversation, Prakash decided to discuss how linear regression could be applied in the context of cricket.

"Hey, Swetha," Prakash started, "you know, we've been talking about machine learning algorithms lately. It's interesting to think about how they could be used in the world of cricket. For instance, consider linear regression."

Swetha, always up for an intellectual conversation, replied, "Oh? How do you think linear regression could be applied here?"

Prakash thought for a moment and said, "Well, let's say we want to predict a batsman's performance based on factors like their batting average, strike rate, and the number of matches they've played. We could use linear regression to build a model that relates these features to the player's total runs scored."

Swetha nodded in agreement. "That's an interesting idea! The model could help coaches and team managers make more informed decisions when selecting players."

Prakash, glad that Swetha was interested in learning more, began explaining linear regression. "Linear regression is a simple yet powerful algorithm used for predicting a continuous target variable based on one or more input features. The idea is to find the best-fitting straight line that describes the relationship between the input features and the target variable."

Swetha listened attentively as Prakash continued, "To do this, the algorithm estimates the coefficients or weights for each input feature. These coefficients represent the strength and direction of the relationship between the input features and the target variable. The best-fitting line is the one that minimizes the sum of the squared differences between the actual target values and the predicted values, also known as the residual errors."

Let's say we want to predict a batsman's total runs scored in a season based on their batting average, strike rate, and the number of matches they've played. We can use a linear regression algorithm to estimate the coefficients or weights for each input feature.

The coefficient for batting average would represent how much each increase in batting average contributes to the total runs scored. For example, if the coefficient is 50, it means that for every point increase in batting average, the batsman can expect to score an additional 50 runs in the season.

Similarly, the coefficient for strike rate would represent how much each increase in strike rate contributes to the total runs scored. If the coefficient is 20, it means that for every one percent increase in strike rate, the batsman can expect to score an additional 20 runs in the season.

Finally, the coefficient for the number of matches played would represent the baseline contribution of simply being on the field. If the coefficient is 100, it means that just being on the field for one match would result in 100 runs being scored in the season.

To find the best-fitting line that minimizes the sum of squared differences between actual and predicted values, the algorithm combines these coefficients in a way that best fits the data.

For example, this will be the linear equation for runs scored.

Total runs scored = 50 * AVG + 20 * SR + 100 * MP

Swetha nodded, understanding the concept. "So, the algorithm tries to find the line that best fits the data, and we can use this line to make predictions for new data points, right?"

"Exactly," Prakash confirmed. "Once we have the coefficients, we can plug in the input features of a new data point to predict its target value. The simplicity of linear regression makes it easy to interpret and implement, which is why it's often used as a starting point in regression problems."

Swetha pondered for a moment before asking, "But what if the relationship between the input features and the target variable isn't linear? Would linear regression still work?"

Prakash smiled, acknowledging the limitation. "That's an important point, Swetha. Linear regression assumes a linear relationship between the input features and the target variable, so if the relationship is more complex, the model might not perform well. In such cases, we can explore other algorithms like polynomial regression, decision trees, or neural networks, which can capture more complex relationships."

Swetha, eager to learn more about different regression techniques, asked, "Prakash, you mentioned polynomial regression. What is that exactly?"

Prakash nodded, happy to explain. "Polynomial regression is an extension of linear regression, used when the relationship between the input features and the target variable is non-linear. Instead of fitting a straight line like in linear regression, polynomial regression tries to fit a curve that best captures the underlying relationship between the input features and the target variable."

He continued, "To achieve this, the algorithm introduces additional polynomial terms in the input features, which allows the model to fit a more complex curve. For example, if we have a single input feature x, instead of modeling the relationship as $y = b0 + b1 * x$, like in linear regression, we could model it as $y = b0 + b1 * x + b2 * x^2$, where x^2 is an additional polynomial term."

Swetha listened carefully and asked, "So, does that mean we can have different degrees of polynomials in the model?"

"Absolutely," Prakash replied. "The degree of the polynomial determines the complexity of the curve. However, it's important to be cautious when choosing the degree, as higher degrees can lead to overfitting, where the model captures not only the underlying relationship but also the noise in the data. This can result in poor performance on new, unseen data points."

Swetha, curious about choosing the right regression technique, asked, "Prakash, how do we know if we should apply linear regression or polynomial regression for a given dataset?"

Prakash considered the question before answering, "That's an important aspect to consider, Swetha. The first step is to visually inspect the data. You can create a scatter plot of the input features against the target variable to get a sense of the relationship between them. If the relationship appears to be linear, linear regression could be a good starting point. However, if you notice a non-linear pattern, polynomial regression might be more suitable."

He continued, "Another approach is to use cross-validation to compare the performance of different models on the dataset. By training and evaluating linear and polynomial regression models with different degrees, you can assess their performance using metrics like mean squared error or R-squared. The model with the best performance can be considered as the most suitable one for the given data."

Swetha nodded, taking in the information. "That makes sense. So, we should start by examining the data visually and then use cross-validation to compare different models. This way, we can find the most appropriate regression technique for the problem at hand."

"Exactly," Prakash agreed. "It's essential to remember that there's no one-size-fits-all solution in machine learning. The choice of algorithm depends on the specific problem and dataset, and sometimes it might be necessary to explore different techniques or even combine multiple models to achieve the best results."

Swetha, curious about the differences between various algorithms, asked, "Prakash, you mentioned the best-fitting line in linear regression, but how is that different from the line that Support Vector Machines (SVM) create?"

Prakash appreciated the question and began to explain, "That's a great question, Swetha. While both linear regression and SVM can involve lines, their objectives and use cases are different. Linear regression is a regression algorithm, which means it's used to predict continuous target variables. It tries to find the best-fitting line that minimizes the sum of the squared differences between the actual target values and the predicted values."

He continued, "On the other hand, SVM is a classification algorithm used for predicting categorical target variables. It aims to find the optimal decision boundary, or hyperplane, that separates different classes in the feature space. The objective of SVM is to maximize the margin between the classes, which is the distance between the hyperplane and the nearest data points from each class, called support vectors."

Swetha nodded, understanding the distinction. "So, linear regression focuses on minimizing the error between predictions and actual values, while SVM focuses on maximizing the margin between classes in a classification problem. Is that correct?"

"Exactly," Prakash confirmed. "Both algorithms have their unique objectives and applications. Linear regression is best suited for predicting continuous target variables, whereas SVM excels at classifying data points into discrete categories."

Prakash continued. "And we could even extend the idea to predicting a team's overall performance based on the individual performance of its players, the team's past records, and other relevant factors."

Swetha chimed in, "It could also be used to analyze the impact of specific conditions, like the type of pitch or the weather, on match outcomes. This information could help teams better prepare for their matches and develop more effective strategies."

As Prakash and Swetha discussed the potential applications of linear regression in cricket, the enthusiasm in their conversation reinvigorated their spirits. They continued to share ideas and explore the possibilities, bringing excitement back into the slower-paced moments of the match. The synergy of sports and data analysis made for a captivating experience, as they eagerly watched the rest of the game unfold.

7

Party Probabilities: Unraveling the Sigmoid Function

Prakash and Swetha were attending a friend's birthday party at a lively rooftop restaurant. The atmosphere was filled with laughter and chatter, as guests enjoyed the evening. As they savored their appetizers, Prakash couldn't help but notice that the restaurant's menu had a peculiar feature: each dish was assigned a "Spiciness Score" from 1 to 10.

Swetha, noticing Prakash's curiosity, chuckled and said, "I bet you're thinking about how to predict the spiciness of a dish using machine learning, aren't you?"

Prakash laughed, slightly embarrassed but impressed by Swetha's intuition. "You caught me! I was actually wondering if logistic regression could be applied here."

Swetha grinned and began explaining, "Logistic regression is perfect for this scenario, as it's a classification algorithm used to predict binary outcomes or classes. In this case, we could use it to predict whether a dish is spicy or not, based on its features like ingredients, cuisine, ordered along with etc."

Prakash, intrigued, asked, "But how does it work? Isn't regression meant for predicting continuous values?"

Swetha replied, "Good question! While linear regression predicts continuous values, logistic regression uses the logistic function, also known as the sigmoid function, to predict the probability of an instance belonging to a particular class. In our spicy dish example, we could assign the class 'Spicy' to dishes with a Spiciness Score of, say, 6 or above, and 'Not Spicy' to those with a lower score."

Prakash asks, "Can you simplify the Sigmoid function for me?"

Swetha smiled, understanding that the sigmoid function might seem a bit complex at first glance.

Imagine you're the manager of a fancy restaurant, and you want to know how full the restaurant is likely to be at any given time. You could use a sigmoid function to predict this!

Now, a sigmoid function is kind of like the way people fill up a restaurant. At the start of the day, there are only a few customers, so the restaurant is pretty empty. As more and more people start coming in, the restaurant fills up quickly at first, but then starts to level off as the night goes on.

This is just like a sigmoid function! The sigmoid function starts off at a low value (the left side of the curve), then increases quickly at first (the steep part of the curve), and then levels off as it approaches a maximum value (the right side of the curve).

So, in restaurant terms, the sigmoid function is like the rush of customers that fills up the restaurant at first, but then tapers off as the night goes on. And just like how you'd use a sigmoid function to predict how full your restaurant is likely to be at any given time, you could use it to predict how many customers you're likely to get throughout the night. Just be sure to save a table for me!

"In technical terms, The sigmoid function, also known as the logistic function, is used in logistic regression to convert a continuous input value into a probability value between 0 and 1. In simpler terms, it helps us determine the likelihood of an instance belonging to a specific class."

She continued, "The sigmoid function has an S-shaped curve, and its formula is given by:

sigmoid(x) = 1 / (1 + e^(-x))

where x is the input value and e is the base of the natural logarithm, approximately equal to 2.718."

Prakash listened attentively, trying to visualize the function. Swetha added, "Imagine that when the input value, x, is a large positive number, the exponent e^(-x) will be close to zero, making the sigmoid function's value approach 1. On the other hand, when x is a large negative number, e^(-x) will be a large number, and the sigmoid function's value will be close to 0. For values around x = 0, the sigmoid function will output a value close to 0.5."

Prakash nodded, beginning to grasp the concept. "Ah, I see! So, it helps us convert any input value into a probability between 0 and 1, which can be used to make predictions in binary classification problems like our spicy dish example."

Swetha confirmed, "Exactly, Prakash! The sigmoid function is a crucial component of logistic regression, as it enables us to predict probabilities and make binary classifications based on the decision threshold we choose."

Prakash nodded, starting to grasp the concept. "I see. So we'd be predicting the probability of a dish being spicy based on its Spiciness Score. But what if the score is right on the borderline?"

Swetha smiled, acknowledging the challenge. "That's where a decision threshold comes in. You can set a threshold, like 0.5, to classify a dish as 'Spicy' if its predicted probability is greater than or equal to the threshold, and 'Not Spicy' otherwise. The choice of threshold can be adjusted based on the specific problem and the desired balance between precision and recall."

Prakash, delighted by Swetha's curiosity, began explaining the differences between logistic regression and decision trees. "In that case, Logistic regression and decision trees are both classification algorithms, but it looks like they have some key differences in how they work and their preferred use cases."

He continued, "Logistic regression, as we discussed earlier, is a linear classifier that uses the sigmoid function to predict the probability of an instance belonging to a particular class. It works best when there's a linear relationship between the input features and the log odds of the target variable. For example, logistic regression might be preferred in cases like predicting customer churn based on usage patterns and demographic information."

"Decision trees, on the other hand," Prakash explained, "are non-linear classifiers that recursively split the data into subsets based on the input features. They create a tree-like structure with nodes representing decisions or tests on the input features, and leaf nodes representing the final class predictions. Decision trees are more versatile and can capture complex relationships between the input features and the target variable. They are often preferred when the data is hierarchical or when the relationships between the input features are not easily captured by linear models. For instance, decision trees might be a better choice for predicting whether a loan applicant is a high or low credit risk based on various financial and personal factors."

Swetha nodded, understanding the distinctions between the two algorithms. "So, logistic regression is more suitable for linearly separable problems, while decision trees are better for capturing complex relationships and handling hierarchical data. Is that right?"

"Exactly," Prakash confirmed. "Each algorithm has its strengths and weaknesses, and the choice depends on the nature of the problem, the dataset, and the desired interpretability of the model. It's essential to carefully consider these factors when selecting the most appropriate classification algorithm for a given problem."

As Prakash and Swetha continued their discussion on logistic regression, they found themselves delightfully distracted from the party's festivities. They joked about using the algorithm to predict the spiciness of their friends' dance moves, all while deepening their understanding of machine learning in a lighthearted and humorous manner.

8
Cluster Capers: Exploring K-means

Prakash and Swetha were at the mall, indulging in a shopping spree. As they wandered through different sections, they couldn't help but notice how the stores were organized according to categories like clothing, electronics, and cosmetics.

Swetha, sensing an opportunity to discuss machine learning, chuckled and said, "You know, this mall's layout reminds me of the k-means clustering algorithm."

Prakash, amused by the comparison, replied, "I've heard of k-means, but I'm not entirely familiar with how it works. Care to explain, using a funny example?"

Imagine you're at a crowded mall, and you're trying to group people based on their clothing styles. You see a bunch of people wearing hoodies and jeans, some people in business suits, and a few eccentric folks wearing brightly colored costumes.

Now, if you wanted to group these people together based on their clothing, you could use K-means clustering! K-means clustering is like playing a game of "Guess Who" with the people in the mall.

You start by picking a number, let's say three, and then you randomly choose three people in the mall as your "centroids" or your "Guess Who" characters. Then, you start grouping people based on their clothing style by asking questions like "Is the person wearing a hoodie?" or "Is the person wearing a suit?"

As you continue to group people, you might find that some people fit better in a different group, so you switch them around until you're happy with the groupings. Once you're done, you can look at each group and see what they have in common, like their clothing style or color choices.

So, just like "Guess Who," K-means clustering is a way to group things together based on their similarities. And just like trying to guess who your opponent has on their card, K-means clustering involves making educated guesses about which group each person belongs to.

Prakash, curious, asked, "But how does the algorithm determine these clusters?"

Swetha explained, "The k-means algorithm starts by randomly selecting 'k' initial cluster centers, or centroids. It then assigns each data point to the nearest centroid. Next, the algorithm updates the centroids by calculating the mean of all data points belonging to each cluster. This process of assigning data points and updating centroids is repeated iteratively until the centroids' positions stabilize, and the clusters don't change significantly between iterations."

Prakash, starting to grasp the concept, nodded and said, "Shall we play the Guess Who game now?"

Prakash and Swetha decide to play the Guess Who game with people in the mall using K-means clustering:

Prakash: "Okay Swetha, let's play a game. Let's try to group these people in the mall based on their clothing styles using K-means clustering!"

Swetha: "Okay, that sounds fun! How many groups should we make?"

Prakash: "Let's start with three groups. I'll pick the first centroid, and then you can pick the next two."

Swetha: "Sounds good! Alright, for my first centroid, I'm going to pick that guy over there in the business suit."

Prakash: "Great choice! For my centroid, I'm going to pick that group of people wearing hoodies and jeans over there."

Swetha: "Okay, for my second centroid, I'm going to pick those people in brightly colored costumes."

Prakash: "Interesting choice! Alright, let's start asking questions to group people together. I'll start: Is the person wearing a hoodie?"

Swetha: "Yes, that person over there is wearing a hoodie."

Prakash: "Great, I'll add them to my group. Okay, your turn. Is the person wearing a suit?"

Swetha: "No, that person over there is wearing a t-shirt and shorts."

Prakash: "Okay, I'll keep asking questions for my group. Is the person wearing jeans?"

Swetha: "Yes, that person over there is wearing jeans and a hoodie."

Prakash: "Excellent, I'll add them to my group. Your turn again."

Swetha: "Is the person wearing a hat?"

Prakash: "No, that person over there isn't wearing a hat."

Swetha: "Okay, let me switch my second centroid to those people wearing hats over there."

Prakash: "Sure thing! Let's keep going. Is the person wearing a tie?"

Swetha: "Yes, that person over there is wearing a tie."

Prakash: "Okay, I'll add them to my group. This is getting fun! Let's pause now."

Prakash raised an eyebrow. "That's interesting! But how do you choose the right value for 'k'?"

Swetha acknowledged the challenge. "Selecting the optimal 'k' can be tricky. One common method is the elbow method, where you plot the sum of squared distances between data points and their cluster centroids against different values of 'k'. You then look for the 'elbow' point, where adding more clusters doesn't significantly reduce the sum of squared distances. In our mall example, it's like finding the optimal number of categories that best organize the people."

Prakash in a deep thought. "but, KNN and K-Means sound so similar"

Swetha grinned, recognizing that the similarity in the names might be confusing. "I can see how you might think that, Prakash. While their names are indeed similar, k-nearest neighbors (kNN) and k-means are quite different in their purpose and how they work."

She continued, "kNN is a supervised learning algorithm used for classification and regression problems. It predicts the output for a new data point by considering the 'k' nearest neighbors from the training data. So, if you have labeled data points and want to classify or predict an output for a new instance, kNN is the way to go."

Swetha then contrasted kNN with k-means, "On the other hand, k-means is an unsupervised learning algorithm used for clustering problems. It aims to partition the dataset into 'k' clusters by minimizing the within-cluster sum of squared distances from each data point to the cluster centroid. K-means is useful when you don't have labeled data and want to discover natural groupings in your dataset."

Prakash nodded, appreciating the clarification. "Ah, I get it now. So kNN is for supervised learning with labeled data, while k-means is for unsupervised learning to find clusters in unlabeled data. Thanks for clearing that up!"

Prakash asked "Now, Can you give some real time examples where K-Means is used?"

Swetha enthusiastically responded, "Certainly! K-means is widely used across various domains for different purposes. Let me give you a few real-world examples where k-means clustering is applied."

Customer segmentation: "Companies use k-means to segment customers based on their purchasing behavior, demographics, or preferences. This helps them create targeted marketing campaigns, develop tailored products, or improve customer service for each group."

Document clustering: "K-means can be used to analyze and cluster large sets of documents, such as news articles or research papers. By grouping similar documents, it becomes easier to discover relevant information, organize the content, and enhance search engine capabilities."

Image compression: "K-means can be applied to image processing, particularly for color reduction and compression. By reducing the number of colors in an image to 'k' representative colors, you can significantly decrease the image size while maintaining the overall appearance."

Anomaly detection: "K-means is used in various industries, such as finance, healthcare, and manufacturing, to detect unusual patterns or outliers in datasets. Identifying these anomalies can help prevent fraud, diagnose diseases, or improve quality control."

Geospatial data analysis: "K-means is used to cluster geospatial data, like analyzing satellite images to identify land use patterns, determining optimal locations for new stores or facilities, or clustering similar geographic regions for resource allocation."

Prakash listened attentively, fascinated by the wide range of applications for k-means clustering. "Wow, it's amazing how versatile k-means is! It seems like clustering can provide valuable insights across many different fields."

Swetha agreed, "Absolutely! K-means is a powerful and flexible algorithm that can be adapted to a variety of situations. It's one of the reasons it's so popular in the world of data science and machine learning."

As they went about their day, Prakash and Swetha continued to exchange examples and ideas about k-means clustering, discovering new ways to apply the algorithm to everyday situations and challenges. Their engaging discussion not only helped solidify their understanding of k-means but also sparked their curiosity about other machine learning techniques.

9

Algorithm Avengers: Unleashing the Random Forests

One weekend, Prakash and Swetha decided to visit a local amusement park. As they wandered through the park, they came across a fortune teller's booth, surrounded by visitors eager to have their fortunes told. This sparked an idea in Prakash's mind.

Grinning, Prakash said, "You know, Swetha, this fortune teller reminds me of the random forest algorithm in machine learning."

Swetha asked, "Really? I'm not very familiar with random forests. How are they like fortune tellers?"

Prakash chuckled and began explaining, "Well, imagine you have a group of fortune tellers, each with their own crystal ball. They all have their unique methods and styles, but they're not perfect individually. However, when you combine their predictions, you get a more accurate and reliable fortune. In a similar way, a random forest is an ensemble of decision trees, each with its own way of making predictions. By combining the results of all these trees, you get a more accurate and robust model."

Swetha, intrigued, asked, "But how does the algorithm create these different decision trees?"

Prakash elaborated, "The random forest algorithm creates a diverse set of decision trees by using two techniques: bagging and feature randomness. In bagging, the algorithm selects random subsets of the training data with replacement to create each tree. For feature randomness, it chooses a random subset of features at each split. This ensures that each tree in the forest is unique, capturing different aspects of the data."

Swetha nodded, "I see. So, it's like a council of fortune tellers, each with their distinct approach, coming together to make better predictions. But how does the random forest make a final decision based on the individual trees' outputs?"

Prakash replied, "For classification problems, the random forest combines the outputs of all trees using a majority vote. So, the class with the most votes is chosen as the final prediction. In the case of regression problems, the algorithm calculates the average prediction of all trees."

Swetha, after pondering for a moment, asked, "Why do we need random forests when we already have decision trees? Isn't it like having a whole team of superheroes when one superhero could do the job?"

Prakash laughed at the analogy and replied, "Well, think of it this way: decision trees are like individual superheroes, each with their own strengths and weaknesses. While a single superhero can save the day in some situations, they might struggle when faced with a more complex or unfamiliar problem."

Swetha chimed in, grinning, "So, you're saying that a random forest is like the Avengers? A group of superheroes coming together to tackle bigger challenges?"

Prakash laughed and nodded, "Exactly! Random forests are like an ensemble of decision trees, or superheroes, working together to make better predictions. While individual decision trees can sometimes overfit the data or be biased towards certain features, the combined power of multiple trees can help overcome these issues. By averaging their predictions, random forests can improve accuracy, reduce overfitting, and create a more stable and reliable model."

Swetha smiled, "Got it! So, even though decision trees are useful on their own, random forests can provide that extra 'oomph' to tackle more challenging problems. Thanks for the fun and enlightening explanation, Prakash!"

Swetha, interested in their superhero discussion, asked, "Alright, Prakash, since we're talking about decision trees and random forests, can you give me a few examples where we would choose one over the other? I want to know when to call in a single superhero and when to assemble the whole team."

Prakash, enjoying the lighthearted tone, replied, "Sure thing! Let's take a look at a couple of scenarios."

Scenario 1 - Decision Tree:

"Imagine you have a small dataset with only a few features, and you're trying to predict whether someone will enjoy a new ice cream flavor. In this case, a single decision tree might work just fine. It's a simple problem, like rescuing a cat from a tree. One superhero, or decision tree, can handle it efficiently without any need for backup."

Scenario 2 - Random Forest:

"Now, let's say you're working on a more complex problem, like predicting the stock market's movement based on a large number of variables. In this situation, relying on a single decision tree might be risky due to overfitting or the tree's inherent bias towards certain features. It's like trying to save the world from an alien invasion – a single superhero just won't cut it. You'd need the entire superhero team, or a random forest, to tackle the problem and make more accurate predictions."

Swetha laughed, "I love the examples! So, for simpler problems with fewer variables, a decision tree can work just fine. But when it comes to more complex problems with many features, it's time to assemble the random forest squad!"

Prakash grinned, "Exactly! It's all about choosing the right superhero, or algorithm, for the task at hand. And remember, you can always experiment with both to see which one gives you better results."

As they continued their day, Swetha and Prakash kept the humor alive by imagining various machine learning algorithms as different superheroes, each with their own set of powers and weaknesses. The playful conversation helped Swetha understand the importance of selecting the appropriate algorithm based on the problem at hand and made their exploration of machine learning techniques all the more enjoyable.

10
Artful Dimensionality: Unraveling PCA

Prakash and Swetha decided to spend their weekend visiting an art gallery featuring an exhibition on modern abstract art. As they stood in front of a particularly chaotic painting, Swetha couldn't help but notice the numerous overlapping colors, shapes, and lines.

Chuckling, Swetha said, "You know, Prakash, this painting reminds me of Principal Component Analysis (PCA) in machine learning."

Prakash, amused by the connection, asked, "Really? How is PCA related to this abstract art masterpiece?"

Swetha smiled and began her explanation, "Well, imagine this painting as a high-dimensional dataset with many overlapping features. It's difficult to understand the underlying patterns or structure, right? PCA is a technique used to simplify complex datasets by reducing their dimensions while preserving as much information as possible. It's like having a skilled artist create a simpler, more interpretable version of this painting."

Intrigued, Prakash asked, "But how does PCA actually do that? How can it simplify a dataset while retaining its essence?"

Swetha explained, "Great question! PCA works by identifying the directions, or principal components, along which the variation in the data is the greatest. It then projects the data onto these new axes, effectively reducing the dimensions. The result is a transformed dataset that's easier to analyze and visualize, much like a less complicated version of this painting."

Swetha continued, "Let's consider this painting as our complex dataset. Imagine that the various colors, shapes, and lines in the painting represent different features of the data. Now, some of these features might be highly correlated, making it difficult to discern any meaningful patterns or relationships."

Prakash listened intently as Swetha continued, "So, PCA would look for directions within the painting that capture the most variation among the colors, shapes, and lines. Think of these directions as new axes, onto which the painting's elements are projected. By doing this, we can reduce the overlapping features and make the painting easier to interpret."

Prakash, starting to grasp the concept, asked, "You mean PCA would create a simplified version of the painting by focusing on the most significant features and removing the less important ones?"

Swetha smiled, "Exactly! By projecting the painting onto these new axes, we create a less cluttered, more interpretable version of the artwork. This simplified painting would still retain the essence of the original but would be much easier to analyze and appreciate."

Prakash chuckled, "I see! So, PCA is like an artistic filter for data, simplifying it without losing its meaning. But how do we decide how many principal components to keep?"

Swetha replied, "That's an important consideration. Ideally, we want to retain enough principal components to capture a significant portion of the original data's variance. One common approach is to use a scree plot, which shows the explained variance for each principal component. By looking at the plot, you can identify the 'elbow point,' where adding more components doesn't provide much additional benefit. That's your cue to stop and strike a balance between dimensionality reduction and information preservation."

Prakash, still thinking about the painting analogy, asked, "Swetha, I'm curious, is PCA considered a machine learning algorithm, or is it something else?"

Swetha replied, "That's an interesting question, Prakash. PCA is not technically a machine learning algorithm in the traditional sense. It's actually a technique for dimensionality reduction and feature extraction. It's used as a preprocessing step to help simplify complex datasets before applying machine learning algorithms. By reducing the number of dimensions, PCA makes it easier for machine learning models to learn patterns, relationships, and structure from the data."

Prakash nodded, "Ah, I see. So, PCA is more like a powerful helper that paves the way for machine learning algorithms to work more efficiently and effectively on complicated datasets."

Swetha smiled, "Exactly! You can think of PCA as an essential tool in the data scientist's toolbox, assisting machine learning models in making sense of high-dimensional data."

Prakash, amused by the idea, asked, "Swetha, let's say I have unlimited memory on the cloud and can store as much data as I want. Why would I still need PCA? Can't I just work with the entire dataset and let my powerful machines handle it?"

Swetha chuckled, "Ah, Prakash, I can see why you might think that. While it's true that having massive computing power and unlimited storage can be tempting, PCA still offers some crucial benefits."

She continued, "Think of it like trying to find a needle in a haystack. Sure, you can have a team of superheroes with X-ray vision, super strength, and telepathy to find the needle, but it would still be easier and more efficient to just reduce the size of the haystack. PCA helps us do just that by simplifying the dataset and making the underlying patterns more accessible."

Prakash grinned, "So, it's not just about how much power and storage we have, but also about making our data more manageable and our machine learning models more effective?"

Swetha nodded, "Exactly! PCA can help improve the performance and interpretability of our models, and it can also reduce computational complexity and training time. In the end, it's about working smarter, not harder."

Prakash laughed, "Got it, Swetha! So even if I have all the computing power in the world, PCA is still my trusty sidekick to streamline the data analysis process."

Prakash, still intrigued by the concept of PCA, asked, "Swetha, let's say someone hands me a dataset. How do I know if I should apply PCA or not? Is there a secret handshake or a magical formula to decide?"

Swetha laughed, "No secret handshake, Prakash, but there are some indicators that can help you determine whether PCA might be beneficial for your dataset."

She continued, "First, consider the dimensionality of your dataset. If you have a large number of features or variables, PCA can help you reduce the dimensions while retaining most of the information. Second, check if there are strong correlations among the features. PCA works well when there's multicollinearity, as it can help identify the underlying structure and simplify the dataset."

Prakash nodded, "Okay, so if my dataset has many dimensions or correlated features, PCA could be my go-to technique. Anything else?"

Swetha added, "One more thing to keep in mind is the performance of your machine learning models. If your models are struggling with high-dimensional data or overfitting, applying PCA might help improve their performance by reducing noise and complexity."

Prakash chuckled, "Thanks, Swetha! With your guidance, I'm now a PCA detective, ready to spot the telltale signs of when it's needed. I promise to use my newfound powers wisely!"

Prakash, with a mischievous grin, asked, "Swetha, one last question. After applying PCA, am I free to choose any machine learning algorithm, or will PCA hold my hand and restrict me from exploring the whole playground of algorithms?"

Swetha laughed, "Prakash, you're quite the character! The good news is, PCA doesn't hold your hand or put any strict limitations on your choice of machine learning algorithms. It's mainly a preprocessing technique to reduce dimensionality and make the data more manageable."

She continued, "Once you've applied PCA, you can experiment with various algorithms to see which one works best for your transformed dataset. In fact, applying

PCA might even make it easier for you to explore a wider range of algorithms, as the reduced complexity of the data can lead to faster training times and improved performance."

Prakash's eyes lit up, "So, PCA is like a friendly guide, helping me navigate the vast world of machine learning algorithms without being overbearing or restrictive. I like that!"

Swetha nodded, "Exactly! PCA is here to help, not hinder. It's a valuable tool that can make your data science journey more efficient and enjoyable."

As Prakash and Swetha wandered through the art gallery, they continued their lighthearted discussions on machine learning, demystifying complex concepts and transforming them into relatable and amusing anecdotes.

11

Branching Out with Hierarchical Clustering

—♡—

Prakash and Swetha were visiting a botanical garden, enjoying the beautiful sights and scents of various plants and flowers. While walking through the garden, Prakash noticed a sign explaining the classification system used for organizing the plant species. Intrigued by this, he turned to Swetha and asked if there were any machine learning algorithms that could create similar classifications.

Swetha, with a twinkle in her eye, said, "Funny you should ask, Prakash! Hierarchical clustering is an algorithm that can do just that. In fact, we can use this garden as a perfect example to explain how it works!"

Prakash, always eager to learn, replied, "Sounds interesting! So, how does hierarchical clustering create these classifications?"

Swetha pointed at the plants around them and said, "Imagine we want to group these plants based on their similarities, like leaf shape, flower color, or even the size of the plant. Hierarchical clustering works by initially considering each plant as its own cluster."

She gestured towards a group of plants with broad leaves and continued, "Let's say we start with these plants here. The algorithm first looks at the similarities between individual plants, such as two plants with similarly shaped leaves. It then merges them into a single cluster."

Swetha then directed Prakash's attention to another section of the garden, where a mix of tall and short plants with various flower colors grew. "Next, the algorithm compares the newly formed clusters with other clusters or individual plants. It might identify a group of tall plants with vibrant flowers as being similar, and merge them together."

As they walked, Swetha pointed to different plant groupings, explaining how the algorithm would continue to merge similar clusters until they reached the top of the hierarchy. "Ultimately, you'll have a tree-like structure, with clusters branching out at different levels, based on their similarities. It's like a botanical family tree, connecting plants with common traits."

Prakash laughed, "Ah, I see! So it's like creating a family tree for plants, where the closest relatives are grouped together first, and then more distant relatives join as we move up the tree."

Swetha smiled, "That's a great way to put it, Prakash! And the best part is that hierarchical clustering can be applied to all kinds of data, not just plants. It's a versatile technique for understanding the relationships within complex datasets."

Prakash, scratching his head, asked, "Swetha, this clustering business has me curious. When it comes to hierarchical clustering, does it work its magic from the top-down like a corporate boss, or does it do the bottoms-up approach like a toast at a party?"

Swetha chuckled, "Well, Prakash, you have quite the imagination! In fact, hierarchical clustering can be both. What I've explained so far is the agglomerative, or bottoms-up approach, where we start with individual plants and merge them into larger clusters. This is like starting with individual party guests and gradually bringing them together for a group toast."

She continued, "On the other hand, there's also the divisive, or top-down approach. In this case, you'd start with all the plants in one big cluster and then keep dividing them into smaller, more specific clusters. It's like a CEO delegating tasks to different departments and then further down to individual employees."

Prakash laughed, "Ah, I see! So, hierarchical clustering can either bring everyone together for a grand celebration or delegate tasks like a strict boss, depending on the approach we choose."

Prakash, with a curious expression, asked, "Swetha, can hierarchical clustering handle any type of dataset thrown at it, like a champion wrestler, or does it have some limitations like a picky eater?"

Swetha smiled at Prakash's amusing analogy and replied, "Well, Prakash, while hierarchical clustering is quite versatile, it does have some limitations. For one, it's not very efficient with large datasets, as the computation can become quite time-consuming. It's like a wrestler who's great at fighting smaller opponents but struggles with the heavyweights."

She continued, "Additionally, hierarchical clustering can be sensitive to the choice of distance metric and the linkage method used for merging clusters. It's important to experiment with different combinations to find the best fit for the data, much like trying out different dishes to satisfy a picky eater."

Prakash, pondering the limitations of hierarchical clustering, asked, "Swetha, let's say I have a massive dataset of customers, like a horde of hungry people at a buffet, and hierarchical clustering is struggling to keep up. What other alternatives do I have to make sense of this chaotic crowd?"

Swetha laughed at Prakash's vivid analogy and replied, "Well, Prakash, when hierarchical clustering can't handle the crowd, there are other clustering algorithms that might be up for the challenge. K-means clustering, for example, is more scalable and can handle larger datasets, like a buffet server who's quick on their feet, efficiently serving everyone in the room."

She continued, "Another option could be DBSCAN, which is a density-based clustering algorithm. It's particularly good at handling datasets with varying densities and finding clusters of different shapes and sizes. Think of it as a master chef who can whip up dishes for all tastes and preferences."

Prakash grinned, "Ah, I see! So, when hierarchical clustering can't keep up with the hungry masses, there are other clustering heroes ready to step in and save the day. Thanks, Swetha!"

With a thoughtful look on his face, Prakash asked, "Swetha, we've been talking about various clustering algorithms, and I'm curious – how do we evaluate the performance of these algorithms? Are there any specific metrics that can help us determine if we've chosen the right one for our data, or is it more like picking our favourite ice cream flavour based on personal preference?"

Swetha smiled at Prakash's ice cream analogy and said, "While personal preferences might play a role in choosing an ice cream flavor, evaluating clustering algorithms is a bit more objective. There are indeed several metrics that can help you assess their performance."

She continued, "Some common metrics include the silhouette score, which measures how similar a data point is to its own cluster compared to other clusters, and the Davies-Bouldin Index, which evaluates the average similarity between clusters. Lower values of the Davies-Bouldin Index indicate better clustering results."

Swetha added, "Another metric is the Calinski-Harabasz Index, which compares the within-cluster dispersion to the between-cluster dispersion. A higher value indicates better clustering performance."

Prakash nodded, "Ah, I see. So, it's not just about personal preference, but more about using these metrics to find the best clustering algorithm for the job. Thanks, Swetha!"

Prakash asked, "Swetha, this hierarchical clustering thing sounds cool, but can you give me some real-life examples where it would be useful? I mean, besides organizing my massive collection of socks by color and pattern."

Swetha laughed, "Well, Prakash, while hierarchical clustering might help you find the perfect pair of socks for every outfit, it also has many other applications! For example, it's widely used in biology to group genes or proteins with similar functions or to build phylogenetic trees for species classification."

She continued, "In the business world, hierarchical clustering can be used to segment customers based on their purchase behaviour, helping companies to target their marketing efforts more effectively. It's also used in document clustering to group similar articles or web pages together, making it easier to find relevant information."

As they strolled through the botanical garden, Prakash and Swetha continued to share amusing insights and real-life applications of hierarchical clustering, making their day both entertaining and enlightening.

12

Boosting Algorithms: The Flavors of Teamwork

One sunny afternoon, Prakash and Swetha decided to visit an amusement park to enjoy some thrilling rides. As they stood in line for the roller coaster, Prakash decided to use the opportunity to explain boosting algorithms to Swetha, relating the concepts to their thrilling adventure.

Prakash, with excitement in his eyes, said, "Swetha, have you heard of boosting algorithms in machine learning? They're kind of like this roller coaster we're about to ride!"

Swetha, curious and slightly nervous about the roller coaster, asked, "Oh, really? How so?"

Prakash explained, "Well, boosting algorithms combine multiple weak learners, like individual roller coaster cars, to form a strong learner, just like the entire roller coaster train. Each weak learner corrects the errors made by the previous one, and they all work together to improve the overall model's performance."

Swetha, intrigued by the analogy, asked, "Prakash, I'm curious to see how it relates to the scary ride I am going to take now!"

"Not this ride, but" Prakash, eager to clarify the concept, looked around and pointed to the carousel. "Alright, let's consider the carousel as a classification problem. Each horse represents a weak learner that's trying to classify whether a person will enjoy the ride or not, based on their age, height, and thrill-seeking preferences."

He continued, "Each horse, or weak learner, makes a prediction, but none of them are very accurate on their own. However, when we combine all the horses, they form a strong learner, like the whole carousel. The boosting algorithm adjusts the weight of each horse's prediction based on its performance, so the better-performing horses have more influence on the final decision."

Swetha laughed, "That's a fun way to think about it! So, the carousel of weak learners works together to give us a better prediction of whether someone will enjoy the ride. Got it!"

Swetha raised an eyebrow and asked, "Prakash, this sounds quite similar to random forests. Are they secretly related, like long-lost amusement park ride siblings or something?"

Prakash replied, "They might seem similar at first, like two thrilling rides in the same park, but they have different approaches. While random forests use multiple decision trees and aggregate their results, boosting algorithms focus on improving the performance of weak learners by iteratively correcting their errors."

He continued with a grin, "Think of random forests as a group of bumper cars, each operating independently and then collectively contributing to the overall result, whereas boosting is more like the carousel we just discussed, where each horse's performance is adjusted based on how well they predict the outcome."

Swetha asked," tell me a bit more about this performance adjustment"

Prakash, sensing Swetha's curiosity, decided to dive deeper into the performance adjustment aspect of boosting algorithms. "Sure, Swetha! In boosting, the performance adjustment is an essential step to improve the accuracy of the overall model."

He continued, "Let's revisit our carousel example. After the first horse makes a prediction, the boosting algorithm calculates the errors it made. The next horse then focuses on correcting those errors by giving more importance to the misclassified instances. This process continues with each subsequent horse, learning from the mistakes of the previous ones."

Prakash added with a smirk, "It's like a team of acrobats, where each member performs their act, and if someone slips or fumbles, the next acrobat steps in to fix the mistake, making the overall performance better with each iteration."

Swetha nodded, "That makes sense! So, the performance adjustment helps each weak learner to focus on the errors made by its predecessors, ultimately creating a stronger model when they're all combined. Thanks for the explanation, Prakash!"

Swetha pondered for a moment and asked, "Does this mean random forests create all models at once, while boosting one after the other?"

Prakash nodded with a smile, "Exactly, Swetha! In random forests, all the decision trees are built independently and in parallel, like a group of enthusiastic kids all trying to build sandcastles at the same time. They don't communicate with each other during the process, but their individual results are combined at the end to produce the final prediction."

He continued, "On the other hand, boosting is more like a team of sandcastle builders working sequentially. Each builder carefully observes the previous builder's work and focuses on fixing any mistakes or weaknesses before adding their own contribution. The final sandcastle, or in our case, the model, is a result of their cumulative efforts, with each builder's work influencing the next."

Swetha laughed, "I love these analogies! They make it so much easier to understand the differences between these algorithms. So, random forests are like independent sandcastle builders, while boosting algorithms work sequentially, like a team. Got it!"

Swetha's eyes widened as she said, "Wait a minute. Boosting seems much smarter than random forests! How does one decide which one to choose?"

Prakash grinned and replied, "Ah, that's the million-dollar question! Choosing the right algorithm depends on the specific problem you're trying to solve and the nature of your dataset. It's like deciding whether to go on a roller coaster or a Ferris wheel; both rides are fun, but they offer different experiences."

He continued, "Random forests usually perform well on most problems and are less prone to overfitting. They can handle large datasets, deal with missing values, and are easier to parallelize. Boosting algorithms, like AdaBoost or Gradient Boosting, are often more accurate, but they can be more sensitive to noise and take longer to train because they work sequentially."

Swetha nodded thoughtfully, "So it's all about understanding the problem and dataset, and then picking the right 'ride' for the job, right?"

Prakash agreed, "Absolutely! And remember, you can always experiment with both and compare their performance to see which one works better for your specific use case."

Swetha furrowed her brow and asked, "So, why do we have so many types of boosting algorithms? Is it like having different flavors of ice cream or something?"

Prakash chuckled at her analogy and responded, "That's a fun way to put it! Yes, there are several boosting algorithms because each one has its own unique approach to improving weak learners. It's like having various flavors of ice cream that cater to different taste preferences."

He continued, "For instance, AdaBoost adjusts the weights of misclassified instances and focuses on them in the next iteration, while Gradient Boosting tries to minimize the overall loss function by learning from the residuals of the previous model. Each algorithm has its strengths and weaknesses, and choosing the right one depends on the problem you're trying to solve and the characteristics of your dataset."

Swetha grinned, "I see! So, it's all about finding the right flavor or algorithm that suits the situation best. Thanks for the explanation, Prakash!"

As they moved closer to the front of the line, Swetha asked more questions about boosting algorithms, and Prakash happily answered, creating a humorous and engaging learning experience amidst the excitement of the amusement park.

13
From Machine Learning to Deep Learning: A Futuristic Leap

Prakash and Swetha had spent weeks diving deep into machine learning concepts and discussing various algorithms. They felt more confident in their understanding and were ready to transition from machine learning to deep learning.

One day, Prakash was babysitting his young nephew at his home when Swetha walked in. He was sitting on the living room floor, surrounded by a bunch of colorful flashcards, each featuring a different animal. Prakash was teaching his nephew how to recognize various animals, and they were having a great time.

Swetha, with a playful grin, chimed in, "Hey, are you helping him classify the animals using machine learning or deep learning?"

Prakash laughed and replied, "Well, I guess you could say I'm using the most advanced neural network there is

– the human brain! But since you've brought it up, it's interesting to think about how machine learning and deep learning could be applied to a task like this."

Swetha sat down beside them and joined the fun. "True! A machine learning algorithm might rely on handcrafted features like the number of legs, the presence of fur or feathers, and so on. But a deep learning model, like a neural network, could automatically learn these features and more from the raw image data."

Prakash added, "That's right! And deep learning models can often achieve much better performance on complex tasks like image recognition. It's amazing how far technology has come. Just imagine – one day, we might have AI-powered apps that can teach kids about animals just as well as, if not better than, we can!"

Swetha, excited about the prospect of learning deep learning, asked Prakash, "So, do you think it's a good time for both of us to take the deep learning plunge?"

Prakash nodded enthusiastically, "Absolutely! With our strong foundation in machine learning and our growing understanding of AI, we're well-prepared to start exploring deep learning. It's a rapidly evolving field with many exciting applications, and it can only enhance our career prospects."

Swetha agreed, "You're right. Deep learning can open up new opportunities for us, and I think it'll be a great investment in our future. Plus, we've been having so much fun learning together that I'm sure we'll enjoy this next step in our journey!"

Swetha, eager to make learning deep learning terminology fun, said, "Let's play the terminology game again! Hand me that deep learning book over there, and I'll shoot a term at you."

Prakash handed her the book with a smile, ready to take on the challenge. "Alright, let's do this! Hit me with your best shot, and I'll try to come up with a fun and easy-to-understand explanation."

Swetha looked at Prakash with a playful grin and said, "Alright, here's your first term: '**Neural Networks**.' Explain it to me in a fun and engaging way!"

Prakash thought for a moment and then began his explanation, "Imagine a bunch of little critters called 'neurons' who live in a magical land called 'Deep Learning Land.' These critters have the power to work together to solve complex problems. They form teams, or 'layers,' and each team has a unique role to play. The first team of neurons receives the raw information, and then they pass their findings to the next team. This process continues through several teams until the final team gives you the answer you're looking for. These little critters, working together in layers, form what we call a 'Neural Network.'"

Prakash took the book from Swetha and flipped through the pages before saying, "Okay, now it's your turn. Explain '**Weights and Biases**' to me in a fun and engaging way."

Swetha thought for a moment and then started her explanation. "Imagine our little neuron critters are a group of chefs trying to perfect their recipe for a delicious dish. They have different ingredients, which are the inputs they receive. Now, the 'weights' are like the importance they give to each ingredient – a pinch of salt or a cup of sugar, for example. The 'biases' are like the chefs' personal preferences or secret ingredients that they always add to make the dish taste even better."

She continued, "These weights and biases are the secret sauce that makes the Neural Network work its magic. They help the chefs, or neurons, to cook up the perfect solution to the problem they're trying to solve. And the best part is, they keep refining their recipe during the training process to make it even better!"

Swetha looked at Prakash curiously and said, "Alright, here's a slightly trickier one: '**Backpropagation**.' Let's see if you can come up with a fun way to explain this one!"

Prakash thought for a moment before starting his explanation. "Imagine the little neuron critters have a massive party at Deep Learning Land. They have to clean up the mess after the party, but they don't know where to start. So, they decide to work together, starting from the last room where the party ended, working their way back to the first room where the party began."

He continued, "As they clean, they find better ways to organize the cleanup process, like finding the most efficient way to pick up trash or wash dishes. These improvements help them clean up faster and more effectively. In the world of neural networks, this is called 'Backpropagation.' It's the process of updating the weights and biases by working backward through the layers of the network, starting from the output layer and moving towards the input layer. This way, the neural network can learn from its mistakes and improve its performance."

Prakash looked at Swetha with a playful grin and said, "Okay, your turn now. Explain '**Fully Connected Layer**' to me in a fun and engaging way!"

Swetha thought for a moment and then began her explanation, "Alright, picture the little neuron critters holding a town hall meeting in Deep Learning Land. They invite every single critter from each of the different neighborhoods, or layers, to come and share their ideas and knowledge. During this gathering, every critter has the chance to talk to every other critter, making connections and exchanging valuable information."

She continued, "In a neural network, a 'Fully Connected Layer' is just like that town hall meeting. It's a layer where every neuron is connected to every other neuron in the previous and next layers, allowing information to flow freely and be combined in various ways. It's like a big brainstorming session where the critters work together to come up with the best solution to the problem they're tackling."

Swetha and Prakash looked at each other, feeling excited about their progress in understanding deep learning terminology. They decided to take their learning to the next level.

Prakash said enthusiastically, "I think we've got a good grasp of the basic terms now. How about we dive into deep learning algorithms next week?"

Swetha agreed, "That sounds like a great idea! We can continue our fun and engaging learning journey together. We've made an excellent team so far, so I'm sure we'll be able to tackle the algorithms just as easily."

With a plan in place, Prakash and Swetha looked forward to the next week when they would delve deeper into the world of deep learning algorithms.

14
Between Neurons and Networks

Prakash and Swetha decided to spend their weekend exploring a new science museum in the city. As they walked through the exhibits, they stumbled upon a life-sized replica of the human brain, complete with colorful lights and interactive displays.

Swetha, excited to share her knowledge, turned to Prakash and said, "Hey Prakash, this is a perfect opportunity to explain neural networks to you! Think of them as an attempt to mimic the structure and function of our brains, but for computers."

Prakash, looking at the impressive brain model, raised his eyebrows and asked, "So, it's like we're trying to create a digital version of our brains. Right?"

Swetha laughed, "Exactly! Neural networks are composed of layers of interconnected artificial neurons. These neurons are inspired by the neurons in our brains, and they process and transmit information in a similar way. It's like having a team of tiny digital brains working together to solve complex problems."

Prakash asked, "So, how are these neural networks connected to the machine learning algorithms we've learned so far?"

Swetha replied, "Neural networks are a subset of machine learning algorithms. While traditional machine learning algorithms, like linear regression or decision trees, rely on handcrafted features and simpler learning techniques, neural networks have the ability to learn more complex representations directly from raw data. This makes them especially powerful for tasks like image recognition, speech recognition, and natural language processing, where the data can be highly dimensional and intricate."

Prakash asked, "But I thought neural networks run the same ML algorithms in parallel. Isn't that true?"

Swetha shook her head, "Not exactly, Prakash. Neural networks are fundamentally different from most traditional machine learning algorithms. While some ML algorithms, like decision trees, can indeed be run in parallel to improve performance or create ensemble models like Random Forests, neural networks are built on a completely different architecture. Instead of executing multiple instances of a single algorithm, neural networks use layers of interconnected artificial neurons to learn from data and make predictions. The learning process in neural networks involves adjusting the weights and biases of the connections between these neurons, which is quite different from the techniques used in traditional ML algorithms."

Prakash thought for a moment and responded, "Ah, so it's like comparing apples to oranges, or in this case, comparing traditional algorithms to futuristic digital brains!"

Swetha grinned, "Exactly! Both traditional ML algorithms and neural networks have their strengths and weaknesses, and they're better suited to different types of tasks. It's important to understand their differences to make the most of the tools at our disposal in the world of machine learning and artificial intelligence."

Prakash grinned and asked, "But how do these 'tiny digital brains' learn from data?"

Swetha explained, "Well, when we train a neural network, we adjust the weights and biases of the connections between neurons. This is done using a process called backpropagation, which is like the neurons playing a game of 'telephone' to figure out who's responsible for any errors in their predictions."

Amused by the analogy, Prakash continued, "So, neural networks are essentially a game of 'telephone' played by our brain's digital doppelgangers?"

Swetha nodded, "That's one way to put it! The more layers and neurons we have, the better the neural network can represent and solve complex problems. But remember, just like in the game of 'telephone', adding too many layers can sometimes lead to confusion and miscommunication."

Swetha decided to explain the simplest neural network, a single-layer perceptron, using a simple example. "Let's consider a basic problem: predicting if a fruit is an apple or an orange based on its color and size," she said.

Prakash listened attentively as Swetha continued, "A single-layer perceptron is the simplest neural network, with just one layer of artificial neurons, also known as perceptrons. Each perceptron receives the input features, in this case, the color and size of the fruit, and it calculates a weighted sum of these inputs along with a bias term. The result is then passed through an activation function to make the final prediction."

Prakash asked, "Is the activation function you mentioned similar to the sigmoid function we discussed in the logistic regression chapter?"

Swetha nodded, "Yes, that's right! The sigmoid function is, in fact, one of the popular activation functions used in neural networks. It maps any input value to a value between 0 and 1, making it particularly useful for binary classification problems. However, there are other activation functions that can be used in neural networks, depending on the specific problem and network architecture."

She continued, "Some other common activation functions include the hyperbolic tangent (tanh), which maps input values to a range between -1 and 1, and the Rectified Linear Unit (ReLU), which sets all negative input values to zero while keeping positive input values unchanged. Each activation function has its own set of characteristics, and selecting the right one can greatly influence the performance of the neural network."

She drew a small diagram on a piece of paper, showing the input features connecting to the perceptron, which in turn connected to the output.

Swetha went on, "For our apple-orange example, the perceptron would receive the color and size as inputs, multiply them by their respective weights, add the bias, and then pass the result through an activation function, like the step function. If the output is greater than a certain threshold, the perceptron might predict the fruit is an apple; otherwise, it predicts it's an orange."

Prakash nodded, "So, in this simple case, the perceptron learns to draw a decision boundary based on the color and size of the fruit to separate apples from oranges?"

Swetha smiled, "Exactly! However, it's important to note that single-layer perceptrons can only learn linear decision boundaries. For more complex problems with nonlinear boundaries, we'd need to use multi-layer neural networks, which have hidden layers between the input and output layers. These more complex networks can learn and represent more intricate patterns in the data."

Prakash seemed impressed, "Ah, I see. So, the activation function plays a crucial role in shaping the neural network's output and learning capabilities. It's fascinating to see how these different components come together to create such powerful learning models!"

Prakash, curious about the next step in their learning journey, asked Swetha, "So, what are some popular neural networks we should know about?"

Swetha quickly listed a few names, "We've got Convolutional Neural Networks, Recurrent Neural Networks, Long Short-Term Memory Networks, Autoencoders, and Generative Adversarial Networks, just to name a few."

Seeing the puzzled look on Prakash's face, Swetha reassured him, "Don't worry, we'll take it one at a time. We'll explore each of these networks in detail and, of course, continue our fun learning approach. It's going to be an exciting adventure!"

With that, they ended their conversation for the day, eagerly anticipating the upcoming week when they would dive deeper into the fascinating world of neural networks and deep learning.

15

Picture Perfect: Demystifying CNN's

Prakash, eager to share his knowledge, started explaining Convolutional Neural Networks (CNNs) to Swetha. "You know, Swetha, I've been learning about CNNs, which are a special type of neural network particularly effective at processing images. Let me give you an example from my own life to help you understand how they work."

Swetha listened intently as Prakash continued, "Imagine I have a huge collection of photos from all our trips and outings. I want to organize them into categories, like nature, cityscapes, and portraits. A CNN could help me with this task."

Swetha asked, "But why the name 'convolution'? What does it have to do with this whole process?"

Prakash grinned and replied, "Ah, that's an interesting question! You know how sometimes we say that two things are 'convoluted' when they're twisted or mixed together, right? Well, in mathematics, 'convolution' is a similar concept - it's a function that combines two other functions in a certain way, resulting in a new, transformed function."

He continued with a funny example, "Imagine we're making a smoothie. You have a list of ingredients, and I have a list of blending speeds. Convolution, in this case, would be like blending the ingredients at different speeds to create a perfect mix. In the context of CNNs, the convolution process combines the input image with the filters, creating feature maps that represent the presence of specific features in the image."

Swetha, "and what is a filter?"

Prakash smiled at Swetha's curiosity and explained, "A filter, also known as a kernel, is a small matrix of numbers that we use in the convolution process. It is applied to the input image by sliding over it, and at each position, it performs an element-wise multiplication with the part of the image it covers. Then, the results of these multiplications are added up to produce a single value in the output feature map."

He continued with a lighthearted analogy, "Think of the filter as a tiny magnifying glass that's examining the image for specific features or patterns, like edges, corners, or textures. When the filter finds a strong match, it 'lights up' the corresponding area in the feature map, telling us that the specific feature is present in that part of the image."

Swetha looked at the beautiful landscape painting on the wall and had a playful idea. "Hey, Prakash, let's pretend we're both layers of a CNN, and we have to process this landscape painting! It'll be a fun way to understand how the layers work together. What do you think?"

Prakash chuckled and agreed, "Sure, that sounds like an interesting way to grasp the concept! So, let's say I'm the first layer, and you're the second layer. As the first layer, I'd focus on detecting low-level features, like the edges and color transitions in the painting. I'd use my 'filters' to find horizontal, vertical, and diagonal lines, as well as subtle shifts in color."

Swetha chimed in, "Alright, then as the second layer, I would take the information you've gathered and start looking for more complex features, like textures, patterns, and shapes. Maybe I'd detect the leaves on the trees, the flow of the river, or the contours of the mountains."

Prakash nodded, "Exactly! And as we move deeper into the network, each layer would extract more abstract and high-level features, such as recognizing the type of landscape, the weather, or even the painting style. Finally, the last layers would use all this information to classify the painting or perform any other required task."

Swetha smiled, "That was a fun exercise! It really helped me understand how the layers in a CNN work together to process and extract meaningful information from images."

Swetha raised a valid question, "Ok, I understand the layers, the filters, but where does the actual learning happen?"

Prakash smiled and said, "Swetha! The actual learning in a CNN happens during the training process when the network adjusts its weights and biases. This learning is achieved through a process called backpropagation and an optimization algorithm, such as gradient descent."

He continued, "In simple terms, when the network makes a prediction, we compare its output with the true label using a loss function. The goal is to minimize the loss function by updating the weights and biases of the network. Backpropagation helps us compute the gradients of the loss function with respect to each weight and bias, and the optimization algorithm updates these parameters accordingly."

Swetha nodded with doubt, "a simpler explanation please"

Prakash thought for a moment and then said, "Imagine a teacher is trying to teach a class of students about different types of animals. The class is divided into groups, and each group acts as a layer in our CNN. Each student in the group acts as a filter, focusing on specific features of the animals like fur, legs, wings, or tails."

He continued, "The teacher shows the first group a picture of an animal, and each student in that group identifies a specific feature. They pass on their findings to the next group. The second group of students then combines the features identified by the previous group and starts recognizing more complex patterns like the body shape, color patterns, or other distinctive traits. This process continues until the last group of students can confidently classify the animal based on the information passed along."

Prakash elaborated further, "Now, let's say there's a group of students who act as the loss function. Their job is to assess how well the final group of students have classified the animal, comparing it to the correct classification. If the prediction is incorrect, the loss function group gives feedback to the previous groups, asking them to adjust their focus or understanding of the features."

"This feedback loop, or backpropagation," Swetha explained, "helps each group of students refine their understanding of the animal features, and they become better at recognizing and classifying animals over time. As the students in each group improve their skills, the entire class learns to identify animals more accurately, just like a CNN adjusts its weights and biases to make better predictions."

Prakash grinned and said, "Well, Swetha, Convolutional Neural Networks have become the go-to tool for a variety of image-related tasks. Here are some fun examples of real-world use cases:

Face recognition: Ever wonder how your smartphone's camera is smart enough to put a cute dog filter on your face? That's CNNs working their magic to recognize and track facial features!

Self-driving cars: CNNs help autonomous vehicles 'see' the road and make sense of their surroundings, so you can sit back and enjoy your ride without worrying about driving – or, in our case, the Bangalore traffic!

Artistic style transfer: Feeling artsy? CNNs can transform your mundane photos into masterpieces in the style of famous painters like Van Gogh or Picasso. It's the perfect way to impress your friends on social media!

Disease diagnosis: CNNs are being used to analyze medical images to detect early signs of diseases like cancer. While it's not exactly funny, it's amazing how technology can help save lives, isn't it?"

Swetha raised an eyebrow and asked, "So, Prakash, are CNNs only meant for images, or can we use them for other types of data as well?"

Prakash replied with a thoughtful expression, "That's a great question, Swetha. While CNNs have been primarily developed for image processing tasks, they can also be used for other types of data that have a grid-like structure, such as audio spectrograms, time-series data, and even some text data when represented in specific ways. However, for non-image data, there are often other deep learning architectures that might be more suitable, like Recurrent Neural Networks for sequences or text data."

Swetha chuckled and said, "Wow, Prakash! Those are some fascinating applications. I never thought that neural networks would have such a wide range of uses. I can't wait to see what other exciting things we can do with CNNs!"

16
Unlocking Memory's Mysteries: Dive into LSTMs

It was a pleasant Friday evening, and Prakash and Swetha were excited to join their friend Deepti for dinner at her beautiful home. Deepti was a data scientist at a healthcare company and had a knack for explaining complex concepts in a simple manner. As they were enjoying the delicious food, Swetha couldn't resist asking Deepti about her work on Long Short-Term Memory Networks (LSTMs).

Swetha started, "Deepti, I've heard you've been working with LSTM networks at your company. Can you help us understand how they work with a practical example from your projects?"

Deepti smiled, "Sure! So, LSTM networks are a type of recurrent neural network (RNN) specifically designed to handle sequences of data, such as time series or natural language. One of our projects involves predicting patient health deterioration based on their vital signs and medical history."

Swetha interrupted, "Hold on a second, Deepti. You mentioned that LSTM networks are a type of recurrent neural network or RNN, but we've only learned about regular neural networks and CNNs. So, what is an RNN?"

Deepti nodded, "Ah, I see! Let me clarify that for you. Recurrent Neural Networks, or RNNs, are a type of neural network designed to handle sequences of data. Unlike regular neural networks or CNNs, which process inputs independently, RNNs maintain a hidden state that can capture information from previous inputs in the sequence. This allows them to learn patterns in the data over time, making them suitable for tasks like language modeling, time series prediction, and other problems where the order of the inputs is important."

Prakash looked around the room, trying to grasp the concept, and then asked, "Can you give a simpler example to help my brain understand RNNs, maybe something from this room?"

Deepti smiled and glanced around the room, spotting a row of decorative plates hanging on the wall. "Sure, let's take the example of these plates. Imagine that each plate represents a moment in time, and they have patterns on them. You want to understand the overall story that these patterns tell when put together in a sequence. A regular neural network or CNN would look at each plate individually, ignoring the order in which they appear. But an RNN would take into account the sequence of plates and how each plate's pattern relates to the previous ones. In doing so, an RNN would be able to capture the complete story that these patterns tell when considered together."

Prakash nodded, finally getting a clearer picture of RNNs and their significance in handling sequences of data.

Prakash chimed in, "How are LSTMs different from regular neural networks in this context?"

Deepti replied, "Great question, Prakash! Unlike regular neural networks, LSTMs can effectively remember patterns over longer sequences of data. This is crucial in healthcare as a patient's medical history and vital signs change over time. Regular neural networks would struggle with this task due to the vanishing gradient problem, but LSTMs can overcome that."

Swetha chimed in, "Deepti, think of us like high school students, so don't mind our interruptions. Can you explain the vanishing gradient problem to us in simpler terms?"

Deepti chuckled and said, "Of course, I understand. Let's try this analogy: Imagine you're in a classroom with a long line of students, and the teacher is passing a message down the line by whispering it into the ear of the first student, who then passes it on to the next, and so on. Each time the message is passed, it gets slightly altered or degraded. By the time it reaches the last student, the message might be completely different from the original. This is similar to the vanishing gradient problem in RNNs. As the network processes longer sequences, the gradients used to update the weights during training can become very small, making it difficult for the network to learn long-range dependencies."

Prakash, intrigued, asked, "So, how does LSTM fix the problem and make sure the last student gets the correct message?"

Deepti responded with a smile, "Great question, Prakash! Let's continue with our classroom analogy. To fix the issue, we provide each student with a notebook that they can use to jot down the essential parts of the message. When passing the message, they can refer to their notes, ensuring the core information remains intact. In LSTMs, this is achieved through a memory cell, which is a kind of 'notebook' that stores and retains important information while discarding less relevant details. This memory cell allows the LSTM to learn and maintain long-range dependencies more effectively than traditional RNNs, mitigating the vanishing gradient problem."

Swetha asked, "Can you give us a specific example of how an LSTM processes real-time data?"

Deepti responded, "Certainly! Let's say we're tracking a patient's heart rate over time. An LSTM can learn to recognize patterns in the heart rate data, such as spikes or drops, and correlate them with the patient's medical history. By doing so, it can predict the likelihood of an adverse event, such as a heart attack, based on the patient's historical data and current vital signs."

Swetha, wanting to understand the practical application, asked, "So, given a scenario, how do we decide if we need to apply CNN or LSTM on a use case?"

Deepti thought for a moment before answering, "That's a great question, Swetha. It mostly depends on the type of data you're working with and the problem you're trying to solve. CNNs are particularly well-suited for tasks involving image or grid-like data, such as image classification, object detection, and even some natural language processing tasks. On the other hand, LSTMs excel at handling sequential data, like time series or text data, where the order of the data matters, such as language translation, text generation, or stock price prediction."

Deepti continued, "It's important to analyze your data and understand the problem requirements before choosing the most suitable model. Sometimes, you can even combine both CNNs and LSTMs in a single architecture if your problem requires processing both spatial and sequential information."

Prakash, curious about Deepti's work experience, asked, "As a healthcare data scientist, can you give us a few more examples of LSTMs you've worked with?"

Deepti smiled and replied, "Sure, Prakash! In my line of work, LSTMs have proven to be quite useful in multiple situations. For instance, I've used LSTMs for predicting the progression of certain medical conditions based on time series data collected from patients. It has also been helpful in analyzing ECG data to detect arrhythmias and other heart-related abnormalities."

She continued, "Another interesting example is using LSTMs for natural language processing tasks in healthcare, such as extracting relevant information from clinical notes or predicting patient outcomes based on their medical history. The sequential nature of text data makes LSTMs a suitable choice for these applications."

Deepti decided to lighten the mood with a little joke. She said, "You know, the other day I was thinking about how neural networks and LSTMs are kind of like our brains when we're trying to remember things. Imagine if we had an LSTM layer to help us remember all the important dates and events in our lives!"

Prakash chuckled and added, "Yeah, especially those birthdays and anniversaries! Maybe we could train a model to send reminders for us, too!"

Swetha laughed and said, "Or even better, train it to remember all the jokes we've heard, so we never run out of them during conversations!"

All three of them shared a hearty laugh, enjoying the lighthearted moment amidst their engaging discussion on LSTMs.

17
Generating Unseen Realities: The Power of GANs

Prakash and Swetha were settling down on the couch, sipping their favorite juices and watching a TV show. That evening's episode featured a talented mimicry artist who was imitating the voices of popular Bollywood artists and weaving together a series of hilarious jokes. As they laughed together, Swetha suddenly had a thought.

Swetha: "Hey Prakash, you know what? This mimicry artist is kind of like the human version of GANs, don't you think?"

Prakash, intrigued by the connection, replied: "Hmm, that's an interesting observation! I guess you're right. The artist is mimicking real voices, and GANs do something similar by generating realistic data based on a given dataset."

Swetha: "Exactly! It's like the artist is the generator, trying to create convincing imitations, while the audience acts as the discriminator, judging if the mimicry is accurate or not."

Prakash: "Haha, I love how we're turning a casual TV show into a machine learning discussion! But you're spot on, Swetha. The artist keeps improving their imitations based on the audience's reactions, much like how GANs learn from the feedback loop between the generator and discriminator."

Swetha: "Alright, Prakash, let's start from the beginning. If we were to explain GANs to someone who's completely new to the concept, how would you do it?"

Prakash: "Sure, Swetha! Let me give it a shot. GAN stands for Generative Adversarial Network. Imagine a GAN as a team of two players, the generator and the discriminator. The generator creates fake data, and the discriminator evaluates the data to determine if it's real or fake."

Swetha: "Oh, like our mimicry artist example!"

Swetha: So are GANs supervised or unsupervised?

Prakash: GANs are actually unsupervised learning models. This means that they don't require any labeled data to learn from. Instead, they learn by trying to find the underlying structure of the data and generate new samples that resemble the original data.

Swetha: That's interesting. So, how does the generator in a GAN know what to generate?

Prakash: The generator in a GAN doesn't really "know" what to generate. It just generates a random noise vector and tries to transform it into something that looks like the real data. The discriminator then tries to distinguish between the real data and the generated data. Over time, both the generator and the discriminator get better at their respective tasks, and the generator learns to generate samples that are indistinguishable from the real data.

Swetha: "Prakash, so far we've been discussing learning from data, but now you're talking about generating data. What exactly does that mean?"

Prakash: "Okay, Swetha, let's say I want to teach you how to draw Mickey Mouse. Imagine that I give you a sketch to start with. You take a look and try to draw your own version."

Swetha: "Oh, I see. So I make an attempt, but the nose is all wrong, right?"

Prakash: "the nose should be round, not oval. You take my feedback, fix the nose, and show me your new drawing."

Swetha: "And then you tell me that Mickey's hands look like toothpicks instead of gloves, right?"

Prakash: "Haha, yes! So you fix the hands and show me the updated sketch. We keep going back and forth, with me pointing out the errors and you fixing them."

Swetha: "So eventually, I become a Mickey Mouse sketching expert?"

Prakash: "That's right! And now that you've mastered the art of drawing Mickey, you can create your own version like a GAN model, maybe a Mickey eating ice cream while riding a unicycle!"

Swetha: "Wow, I never thought I'd be able to draw Mickey doing a circus act. Thanks, GANs!"

Swetha: "So, instead of learning to predict something, GANs are creating new, realistic data?"

Prakash: "Exactly! The idea is to create new data points that look and feel like the original data but are not exactly the same. This can be useful in various scenarios, such as creating new images, sounds, or even text that resemble real-world examples."

Swetha asks, "I heard my friend talk about the connection between auto encoders and GANs. Can you explain what are auto encoders and how are they related to GANs?"

Prakash responds, "Auto encoders are also a type of neural network, but they are used for unsupervised learning. They are designed to take an input and generate a compressed representation of it. The compressed representation can then be used to reconstruct the original input with a minimal loss of information."

Swetha asks, "So are autoencoders some kind of PCA that compresses the information?"

Prakash responds, "Well, in a way, yes. Autoencoders are a type of neural network that can be used for unsupervised learning. They work by compressing the input data into a lower-dimensional representation and then reconstructing the original data from this compressed representation. So, you can think of them as a kind of data compression algorithm."

Swetha nods her head in understanding and says, "Okay, I see. But how are they related to GANs?"

Prakash continues, "The generator network in a GAN is actually an autoencoder that's been modified to generate new data. Instead of simply compressing and reconstructing the input data, the generator network in a GAN is trained to generate new data that's similar to the input data, but not identical. So, autoencoders are a fundamental building block for GANs."

Swetha looks fascinated and says, "Wow, that's really interesting! So it's like the generator network is learning how to create new data by analyzing and compressing the existing data, and then using that knowledge to generate new data?"

Prakash nods, "Exactly! It's a really powerful technique, and it's been used in a variety of applications, from generating realistic images to improving speech recognition systems."

Swetha smiles and says, "I'm really starting to see how all of these different deep learning techniques are connected to each other. It's like they're all different tools in a toolbox, and you just need to know when to use each one."

Swetha: "So, apart from generating some hilarious jokes or circus-worthy Mickey Mouse sketches, I'm struggling to see the real-life benefits of GANs. What do you think, Prakash?"

Prakash: "Well, Swetha, GANs have plenty of practical applications beyond just fun and games. They can be used for image synthesis, creating realistic images from scratch, and even improving low-resolution images. They're also used for generating new medical data, simulating complex systems, and even creating realistic virtual environments for training AI models. So, you see, GANs have a wide range of real-life applications that can truly make an impact!"

Swetha: So what should be my judgement point, when should I be thinking of using a GAN vs LSTM vs CNN given a deep learning use case?

Prakash: It depends on the type of data you're working with and what you're trying to achieve. GANs are great for generating new data, while LSTMs are good for sequential data like text or time series. CNNs are ideal for image and video data. You need to look at the problem you're trying to solve and determine which type of network is best suited to the task.

Swetha: I see, so it's not just about using the latest technology but understanding which technology is best suited to the problem at hand.

Prakash: Exactly. It's important to remember that deep learning isn't a one-size-fits-all solution. You need to choose the right tool for the job. And sometimes, it might be a combination of different types of networks.

Prakash chuckles and says, "Exactly! And like any good craftsman, you need to know how to use each tool properly to get the job done right."

Swetha laughs and says, "Well, I'm definitely learning a lot from you, Prakash. Thanks for explaining all of this to me!"

Swetha nods, "I see. So, can we use auto encoders instead of GANs in certain use cases?"

Prakash replies, "Yes, that's possible. Auto encoders are useful for generating data that is similar to the input data, but they may not be able to generate new samples that are entirely different from the input data, like GANs can. So it really depends on the specific use case and the desired outcome."

Swetha: That makes sense. Thank you for explaining that.

Prakash: Anytime, Swetha. And don't forget, we still have a lot to learn. Who knows what exciting new developments are just around the corner?

Swetha: Yes, it's definitely an exciting field to be in.

They continued watching the show, enjoying the humor while also appreciating the fascinating connection between the mimicry artist and GANs. Little did they know that their casual conversation would spark a deeper interest in exploring the world of machine learning even further.

18

Reinforcement Love Through Trial, Error, and Rewards

Swetha and Prakash sat down for their next study session, ready to explore reinforcement learning. Swetha began with an engaging scenario to help illustrate the concept.

Swetha: "Alright, Prakash, let's imagine a scenario to understand reinforcement learning. Think of a little robot dog that's learning to fetch a ball. It has no prior knowledge of how to do it, so it learns by trial and error. Each time the robot dog gets closer to the ball or successfully fetches it, it receives a 'reward' signal. And if it goes in the wrong direction or doesn't fetch the ball at all, it gets no reward or even a negative signal."

Prakash listened attentively, intrigued by the scenario, and asked a question to clarify his understanding: "So, the robot dog is basically learning from its actions and the feedback it receives, right?"

Swetha: "Exactly! In reinforcement learning, an agent – like our robot dog – learns to make decisions by interacting with its environment, receiving feedback in the form of rewards or penalties, and adjusting its actions accordingly to maximize the cumulative rewards."

Prakash, still curious about the concept, asked another question: "So who gives the reward to the robot dog in this scenario?"

Swetha: "In reinforcement learning, the reward is typically provided by the environment itself, which is programmed to give feedback based on the agent's actions. For our robot dog, the environment could be a virtual simulation or a real-world space with sensors that track the dog's movements and proximity to the ball. As the robot dog takes actions, the environment evaluates the outcomes and assigns rewards or penalties accordingly. This feedback loop helps the robot dog learn the most effective actions to maximize its rewards."

Prakash, intrigued by the concept, asked another insightful question: "Looks like the environment is playing a big role here. How can we construct the environment in the first place?"

Swetha: "You're right, the environment is crucial in reinforcement learning. Constructing an environment depends on the problem you're trying to solve. In some cases, you can use a simulated environment, which is a virtual representation of the real world or a simplified model, to train the agent. This can be done using various tools and frameworks, like OpenAI's Gym, for example."

She continued, "For other problems, you might need to create a real-world environment with sensors and actuators that allow the agent to interact with its surroundings and receive feedback. This can be more challenging, as you need to ensure the agent's safety and deal with the complexities of the real world. But in both cases, the key is to provide the agent with clear and meaningful feedback, so it can learn to make better decisions over time."

Prakash raised another concern, asking, "But it seems like an overfitting problem. If the dog is only trained in that specific environment, how would it perform in other new environments?"

Swetha: "That's a valid concern. In reinforcement learning, overfitting can indeed occur if the agent becomes too specialized in a particular environment and fails to generalize well to new situations. To address this issue, we can use various techniques, such as training the agent on a diverse set of environments or using techniques like domain randomization, where we randomize certain aspects of the environment during training to encourage the agent to learn more general strategies."

She added, "Another approach is to use transfer learning, where the agent learns from a source environment and then fine-tunes its knowledge in a target environment. This can help the agent adapt more quickly to new situations, improving its ability to generalize."

Prakash: "That's interesting! But how does the robot dog know which actions to take in the first place?"

Swetha: "The robot dog starts with a set of possible actions, like moving forward, backward, or turning. It initially takes random actions, and as it receives feedback, it updates its knowledge about which actions lead to better rewards. Over time, it learns a policy – a strategy for choosing actions – that allows it to fetch the ball more efficiently and consistently."

Prakash, interested in the practical applications of the concept, asked, "So what are some real use cases of reinforcement learning?"

Swetha: "Reinforcement learning has a wide range of applications across various domains. Some examples include:

Robotics: Reinforcement learning can be used to teach robots to perform complex tasks like grasping objects, walking, or flying, by learning through trial and error.

Finance: Reinforcement learning can help optimize trading strategies or asset allocation in the financial industry by learning to make decisions that maximize profits and minimize risks.

Healthcare: Reinforcement learning can be used to personalize treatment plans for patients, optimizing the choice of medications or therapies based on individual responses and outcomes.

Autonomous vehicles: Reinforcement learning can help self-driving cars learn to make safe and efficient driving decisions by interacting with their environment and adapting to different traffic conditions and road situations.

Gaming: Reinforcement learning has been used to train AI agents that can play and excel at games like Go, chess, and poker, by learning to make strategic decisions that maximize their chances of winning."

Prakash, intrigued by the finance use case, asked, "Let's talk about the finance use case you mentioned. How would you create the environment for that?"

Swetha: " In the finance use case, the environment would be a representation of the financial market, which includes stock prices, trading volume, and other relevant information. To create this environment, we would need to collect historical financial data, such as stock prices and market indicators, and use it as the basis for simulating market dynamics."

She continued, "The agent, in this case, would be an algorithm that learns to make trading or investment decisions. It would interact with the simulated environment by taking actions like buying, selling, or holding assets. The environment would then provide feedback in the form of rewards or penalties based on the agent's actions and their impact on the portfolio value or other performance metrics."

Swetha added, "To ensure the agent can generalize well to new market conditions, we can introduce randomness or variations in the training environment, such as changes in market trends, volatility, or even simulate different types of market events like crashes or bubbles."

Prakash, considering the computational requirements, asked, "So do we need a special setup to train reinforcement learning algorithms? It doesn't look like I can use my laptop."

Swetha: "You're right, training reinforcement learning algorithms can be computationally intensive, especially for large-scale problems or when using complex neural networks. While it's possible to train simpler models on a personal laptop, for more advanced applications, you might need a more powerful setup."

She continued, "This could include using high-performance computers or workstations with powerful GPUs, which can significantly speed up the training process. Another option is to use cloud-based services, like Google Colab, AWS, or Azure, which provide access to powerful computing resources on a pay-as-you-go basis. This allows you to train your reinforcement learning algorithms without the need for expensive hardware investments."

Prakash asked "Can you quickly explain the types of Reinforcement algorithms?"

Swetha nodded and replied, "Sure, Prakash. Reinforcement learning algorithms can be broadly divided into two categories: model-free and model-based."

She continued, "Model-free algorithms don't rely on any underlying model of the environment, so they learn directly through trial and error. The most popular model-free algorithms are Q-learning and SARSA. Both algorithms use a value function to estimate the expected rewards for each state-action pair."

"Model-based algorithms, on the other hand, create a model of the environment to predict the next state and the expected reward. They use this model to decide the best action to take. Some examples of model-based algorithms include Monte Carlo Tree Search and Dyna-Q."

Swetha paused, smiled, and added, "Remember our party analogy? Imagine you're a guest at the party trying to find the best conversation group. Model-free is like jumping into conversations and learning which groups are enjoyable based on trial and error. Model-based would be like observing the groups from afar, making predictions about which groups seem interesting, and then deciding which group to join based on that information."

As their conversation was coming to an end, Prakash decided to lighten the mood with a joke that tied together their relationship and reinforcement learning.

Prakash: "Hey Swetha, you know what? I just realized that our relationship is a lot like reinforcement learning!"

Swetha, intrigued, asked, "Oh really? How so?"

Prakash grinned and replied, "Well, think about it. We started out not knowing much about each other, and through trial and error, we've learned how to make each other happy by taking the right actions. Just like reinforcement learning, we've discovered the best 'policies' for a successful relationship, and we continue to learn and adapt as we grow together!"

Swetha laughed, appreciating the clever comparison. "That's so true, Prakash! We're like the perfect reinforcement learning agents, navigating the environment of love and life together!"

As they shared a laugh, their unique learning journey continued to bring them closer, both in terms of knowledge and their relationship.

19

United by Data Science: A Promising Future Together

As Prakash and Swetha sat in the office cafeteria, they overheard two data scientists arguing about a machine learning use case.

Data Scientist 1: "Alright, so we have this use case where we need to predict customer churn based on their behavior and interactions with our platform. I think we should use a Decision Tree algorithm for this problem. It's simple, interpretable, and can handle both continuous and categorical features."

Data Scientist 2: "Hmm, I see your point, but I believe a Support Vector Machine would work better in this case. It's more powerful, and it can handle high-dimensional data more effectively. Plus, with the right kernel function, we can even capture complex relationships in the data."

Data Scientist 1: "But the interpretability of the model is important for the business team. They want to understand the decision-making process behind the predictions. That's where a Decision Tree has an advantage over a Support Vector Machine."

Data Scientist 2: "True, but we can't sacrifice accuracy for interpretability. The Support Vector Machine can provide a better balance between both. And I think with some explanation, we can help the business team understand the logic behind our choice."

Data Scientist 1: "I still believe a Decision Tree would be better for this use case. It's less sensitive to outliers, and it's easier to visualize and communicate the decision-making process to stakeholders."

Data Scientist 2: "Well, I'm not convinced. A Support Vector Machine can handle the complexity of this problem better, and it's less prone to overfitting, especially with the right regularization parameters."

As the data scientists continued their debate, Prakash and Swetha listened carefully, realizing that both of them were missing the mark in their choice of algorithms. This was the point at which they decided to chime in and offer their suggestion.

Swetha whispered to Prakash, "Should we chime in and save them from their algorithmic blunders?"

Prakash grinned, "Definitely! Let's make this fun and enlightening."

Prakash stood up and addressed the data scientists, "Excuse us, but we couldn't help but overhear your discussion. May we offer a humble suggestion?"

Data Scientist 1, slightly annoyed, replied, "Alright, go ahead. Let's hear your algorithmic wisdom."

Swetha chimed in with a smile, "Well, we believe that a Random Forest algorithm would be better suited for your use case. It's like having an ensemble of decision trees partying together, each with its own unique perspective on the problem, ultimately making a more informed decision than a single tree or a moody Support Vector Machine."

Data Scientist 2 raised an eyebrow, "Interesting. But why would a Random Forest be better?"

Prakash explained, "In this case, it seems like you're dealing with a high-dimensional problem with lots of features. A single Decision Tree might overfit the data, while a Support Vector Machine could struggle with the complexity. A Random Forest, on the other hand, would combine multiple decision trees to make a more robust prediction, reducing overfitting and handling complexity better."

The data scientists looked at each other, considering the suggestion. Data Scientist 1 finally admitted, "You know, that's actually a pretty good point. I guess we were barking up the wrong algorithm trees."

Data Scientist 2 chuckled, "Seems like we've been outsmarted by a pair of ML maestros. Thanks for your input, you two!"

Prakash and Swetha smiled, satisfied that they had contributed to a better solution, and returned to their table, ready to take on more machine learning challenges together.

Prakash and Swetha stepped out of their office building, feeling thrilled about their successful day at work. As they began walking towards their home, they were greeted by the chaos of Bangalore's bustling streets. The air was thick with pollution, making it difficult to breathe, and the constant honking of vehicles drowned out any attempt at conversation.

As they made their way through the crowded streets, they had to navigate around potholes and piles of dirt that seemed to have taken over the roads. The traffic was never-ending, with vehicles of all shapes and sizes jostling for space on the narrow streets.

Despite the challenging conditions, Prakash and Swetha remained in good spirits. They were determined to make the most of their evening, even if it meant shouting to be heard over the noise of the traffic. Little did they know, the obstacles they faced on their walk home would be nothing compared to the challenges that lay ahead.

Swetha: "Hey Prakash, I've got a challenge for you! Let's imagine a problem that India is facing right now and think about how we can implement a solution using deep learning. Ready?"

Prakash: "Sounds interesting! What's the problem you have in mind?"

Swetha: "Well, you know that air pollution is a significant issue in many Indian cities, right? How about we come up with a deep learning solution to predict air pollution levels and help authorities take proactive measures?"

Prakash: "That's a great idea! Let's start by thinking about the data we would need. We'd probably want to gather historical data on air quality, weather conditions, and traffic patterns in the affected cities."

Swetha: "Exactly! And we can use that data to train a deep learning model like a Recurrent Neural Network (RNN) or Long Short-Term Memory (LSTM) model to capture the temporal relationships between the different factors affecting air pollution."

Prakash: "I like the LSTM idea because it can handle long-term dependencies in the data more effectively. Once we've trained the model, we can use it to predict air pollution levels in the future, say, for the next week or month."

Swetha: "Right! And with those predictions, authorities can implement preventive measures, like traffic restrictions or industrial emission controls, to reduce pollution levels. They could also use the predictions to alert citizens and advise them to take necessary precautions like wearing masks or staying indoors on high pollution days."

Prakash: "What a fantastic idea! Deep learning could really make a difference in tackling air pollution in India. We should definitely share this with our colleagues and see if we can collaborate with the right stakeholders to bring this solution to life."

Prakash: "Alright, let me think of an image processing problem that could benefit India. How about using deep learning to identify and classify waste materials in landfills? This could help improve waste management and recycling efforts."

Swetha: "That's an excellent idea! So, how do you propose we implement this solution?"

Prakash: "We can start by collecting a large dataset of images containing various types of waste materials, like plastic, glass, paper, metal, and organic waste. The dataset should be diverse and representative of the waste materials commonly found in Indian landfills."

Swetha: "Once we have the dataset, we can use it to train a Convolutional Neural Network (CNN) to classify waste materials. CNNs are great for image processing tasks, as they can automatically learn to detect patterns and features in the images."

Prakash: "Exactly. After training the CNN, we can deploy it to processing plants, where it can be integrated with cameras or other imaging devices. As waste materials pass through the conveyor belt, the CNN can analyze the images in real-time and classify the waste materials."

Swetha: "That would make the sorting process more efficient and accurate! With better waste classification, recycling plants can recover valuable resources more effectively, and waste management companies can optimize their landfill operations."

Prakash: "In addition to that, the deep learning model could be used to identify hazardous waste materials that shouldn't be mixed with regular waste. This can help prevent environmental and health hazards."

Swetha: "It's amazing how deep learning can potentially improve waste management in India."

Prakash: "Alright, let's think of a problem where reinforcement learning can benefit India. How about using it to optimize traffic management and reduce congestion in urban areas?"

Swetha: "That's a great idea! Traffic congestion is a significant issue in many Indian cities. So, how do you propose we implement this solution?"

Prakash: "We can start by creating a simulation environment of an urban traffic network, including roads, intersections, and traffic signals. We can feed real-world traffic data into the simulation to model the traffic flow accurately."

Swetha: "Once we have the simulation environment set up, we can use a reinforcement learning algorithm, such as Deep Q-Network (DQN) or Proximal Policy Optimization (PPO), to learn how to control traffic signals more efficiently."

Prakash: "Exactly. The reinforcement learning agent can learn to adjust the traffic signal timings to minimize congestion and maximize the overall flow of vehicles through the network. The agent receives rewards for reducing wait times at intersections and penalties for causing traffic jams."

Swetha: "As the agent learns from the simulation, it can adapt its strategies and become more efficient at managing traffic. Once we have a well-trained agent, we can deploy it to real-world traffic management systems and observe its performance."

Prakash: "By optimizing traffic signal timings, we could potentially reduce congestion, improve fuel efficiency, and decrease air pollution. The reinforcement learning agent could even be adapted to handle special situations, like prioritizing emergency vehicles or managing traffic during large events."

Swetha: "I love this idea! Reinforcement learning can indeed help tackle traffic congestion in India."

Swetha: "Let's see, how about using Generative Adversarial Networks (GANs) to help preserve and promote India's cultural heritage and traditional art forms?"

Prakash: "That's an interesting idea! How do you propose we implement this solution?"

Swetha: "First, we need to collect a large dataset of traditional Indian artworks, such as paintings, sculptures, textiles, and handicrafts. The dataset should be diverse and represent various art styles and techniques from different regions of India."

Prakash: "Once we have the dataset, we can use it to train a GAN, which consists of two neural networks – a generator and a discriminator. The generator learns to create new, unique pieces of art that resemble the original dataset, while the discriminator learns to differentiate between real and generated artworks."

Swetha: "As the GAN learns and improves, it can generate high-quality, authentic-looking Indian art pieces.

These generated artworks can be used to create digital galleries, virtual reality experiences, and educational materials that help preserve and promote India's cultural heritage."

Prakash: "That's a great way to use GANs for a good cause! By generating new pieces of art, we can also inspire artists and designers to explore traditional Indian art forms and incorporate them into modern designs, thus ensuring that these art forms remain relevant and appreciated."

Swetha: "Exactly. GANs can also be used to restore damaged artworks, fill in missing portions, or even colorize black and white photographs of historical events, monuments, or people, helping us better understand and appreciate India's rich history and culture."

Before they knew it, they were approaching their home. Swetha paused for a moment, looked into Prakash's eyes, and expressed her gratitude for him being the perfect partner in this learning journey. Their combined efforts and support had made them both extremely confident about embarking on successful careers in the fascinating field of data science.

In conclusion, the journey of Prakash and Swetha through the world of machine learning and deep learning has revealed numerous possibilities and opportunities for harnessing the power of artificial intelligence to tackle pressing challenges in India. From using machine learning algorithms to solve real-world problems to exploring the potential of deep learning techniques like neural networks, GANs, and reinforcement learning, they have uncovered a plethora of innovative solutions that can positively impact various aspects of life in India.

Their discussions have highlighted the potential of AI in improving traffic management, preserving and promoting

India's rich cultural heritage, optimizing agricultural practices, enhancing healthcare services, and much more. These examples serve as a testament to the transformative power of AI and its ability to drive sustainable growth, improve the quality of life, and foster innovation across the nation.

As India continues to embrace technology and digital transformation, the potential for AI-based solutions is immense. By fostering a culture of innovation, investing in research and development, and encouraging collaboration between academia, industry, and the government, India can harness the power of AI to create a better future for its citizens.

Hope the story of Prakash and Swetha serves as an inspiration for individuals, organizations, and policymakers alike, highlighting the importance of continuous learning, creative problem-solving, and the pursuit of innovative solutions to address the diverse challenges faced by the nation. By embracing the power of AI, India can unlock new avenues of growth, prosperity, and well-being for its people, paving the way for a brighter and more resilient future.

Thankyou

Dear Reader,

Thank you for joining Prakash and Swetha on their humorous and enlightening journey through the world of machine learning algorithms. I sincerely hope that "Algorithm Diaries" has provided you with an enjoyable and accessible introduction to data science concepts while also sparking your curiosity to explore further.

Your feedback is invaluable to me as an author, and I would be delighted to hear your thoughts on the book. Whether you have suggestions for improvement, questions, or simply wish to share your own experiences in the world of data science, please do not hesitate to reach out to me at mkalicharan@gmail.com. Hearing from readers like you is truly one of the greatest joys of writing.

Once again, thank you for your time and for embarking on this adventure with Prakash and Swetha. I wish you all the best in your future endeavors, and I hope that their story has left you inspired and entertained.

Warm regards,
Kalicharan Mahasivabhattu